Something Worth

An Important Message from the Apostle Paul's Letter to the Ephesians

Contents

Foreword 4

Introduction 6

Part One: The Need For The Christians' Armour Explained 8

    Chapter One: The Need To Be Strong 23

    Chapter Two: The Nature Of Our Strength 27

    Chapter Three: The Wiles of The Devil 33

    Chapter Four: For We Wrestle 48

    Chapter Five: The Prince and Power of Darkness 54

Part Two: The Nature of The Christians' Armour 62

    Chapter One: The Centrality of Truth 62

    Chapter Two: The Breastplate of Righteousness 76

    Chapter Three: The Gospel of Peace 85

    Chapter Four: A Good Time to Pause and Reflect 99

    Chapter Five: The Shield of Faith 104

    Chapter Six: The Fiery Darts of The Wicked One 116

    Chapter Seven: The Helmet of Salvation or Keeping Our Head!.. 120

    Chapter Eight: The Sword of The Spirit 125

    Chapter Nine: Praying Always With All Prayer 133

    Chapter Ten: Supplication For All The Saints 138

Conclusion 142

Foreword

In this, his latest book, Stuart Pendrich reminds believers of some of the difficult and undesirable consequences, at least in this life, of choosing to follow Christ. You see, there is a down side to becoming a Christian. (Did the person who led you to Christ forget to tell you about that?) When we repent, and believe the gospel, when we choose to follow our Lord, we are instantly transferred from the kingdom of darkness to the kingdom of light. Our ultimate destination changes from hell to glory with God forever. But for the remainder of our life on this earth, all those who have hated Jesus Christ now hate us also (John 15:18f). And the "god of this world" (2 Cor 5:4), is prowling around like a roaring lion looking to devour us (1 Pet 5:8). As believers, we now have enemies, lots of them. And the "temporary" god of this world is not pulling any punches because he knows that his time is short.

While most of contemporary American preaching has been seduced into superficial pablum and dealing with felt needs, Paul, and Stuart, remind us that we are involved in an all-out war. It is a war "not of our choosing", but it is war never-the-less. As Christians, we are at war not because we hate the world and want to destroy those who are not Christians. We are at war because the unbelieving world hates us and wars against the truth we believe and proclaim. Those of us who belong to Christ are hated by this world and the god of this world, just as Christ is. For this reason, much of this life on earth is a life of warfare.

So how do we fight this battle? In Stuart's book, Something Worth Fighting For, he observes first that our real enemy is not other human beings. The real enemy is the "god" of this world whom we cannot see. He is a spiritual being and his army is also, the fallen angelic creatures. Secondly, because the battle is spiritual and not physical, we must use the armor and weapons God provides, not the normal human arsenal. From Ephesians chapter six, Stuart expounds the purpose, the means and the methodology for conducting spiritual warfare.

Introduction

As I settle down to write an introduction to this latest book, we find ourselves in the throes of yet another war, this time with a deadly virus which seems to know no boundaries. I refer, of course, to the Corona virus, an illness which poses a serious threat to the world of our day, having reached global preportions in a very short psace of time. President Trump has called it our invisible enemy, an enemy we will fight and an enemy we will, in time defeat.

This is not a war we have sought, nor one we welcome; few wars are. However, it is a battle we cannot ignore. It is a conflict in which we all need to play our part if this enemy is to be beaten and we are to overcome it. This is not a time for inaction but a time for everyone of us to play our part whateve that part may be.

The following short study of this closing passage at the end of the apostle Paul's letter to the Christians in Ephesus (Ch. 6:10-18) may not be one of our favorite passages of scripture; nevertheless, it provides a timely reminder to the Christian Church of our day that we too are engaged in an even more serious conflict with even more serious and eternal consequences.

In the years prior to the second world war the British people and the British Parliament paid little heed to the warnings of Sir Winston Churchill writing him off as over reacting to the building up of arms in Germany. They could not believe, far less contemplate, another world war so soonafter the awful conflict of 1914 -1918. This 'unwillingness' cost the nations of our world dearly.

It is a deep seated conviction of this former pastor that the Churches of our day are guilty of a similar and more serious failure to take seriously our danger from the spiritual enemies that threaten us and, more importantly, our duty to put on our spiritual armour which the Lord has provided for His people. The result of this failure is that many Christians and many Churches are not as aware of this conflict as they ought to be to the great cost of the Christian Church and to their own personal blessing.

Part One: The Need For The Christians' Armour Explained

Although my heartfelt concern in what follows is with the issue raised by the Apostle Paul in his letter to the Christians in Ephesus, (which I will refer to in a moment), I have decided to concentrate my attention upon the closing appeal or exhortation found in this final section of the epistle (Ch. 6:10-18) since, in these verses, we find the apostle exhorting the Christians to put on the whole armour of God, in order for them to be able to stand against the wiles of the devil. My reason for doing so is that I hold this to be, not only the conclusion of the letter, but, in a very real sense, the great climax, if not, the very heart of the apostle's message to the Christians in Ephesus and through them to the Christian Church as a whole.

During my years in the ministry (1972 – 2014), I have seen a number of changes taking place, both within the Christian Church itself and in the unbelieving world around us. The latter, to say the least, have been quite disturbing but, nevertheless, somewhat predictable. As we see from the biblical record, God's people have always had a restraining influence upon the ungodly until, that is, they too begin to fall back into sin and unbelief. As the Lord said to His disciples in Matthew, "You are the salt of the earth" (verse 13) until, that is, the salt loses its' savour. Unfortunately, this has all too often been the case, as we see from a reading of the Old Testament and the recorded history of Gods' people, as well as from the story of the Christian Church from the time of Christ to the present day; for in both accounts we constantly see what occurs when God's people are left to themselves. Our nature, apart from God's grace is sinful and whenever the Lord withdraws His hand the tendency in man is always downward as we see from the Apostle's letter to the Romans and the opening chapter. It is, therefore, those subtle changes within the Church that disturb me most of all. In the words of Henry Frances Lyte, (who wrote the words to that once well known hymn "Abide with me"), "change and decay in all around I see."

A large part of my concern is with the current desire to be 'relevant, up to date and modern' as we have tended to make changes which have not always been beneficial to those of us who seek to engage in worship on a Sunday. Indeed, I am somewhat concerned about the hymns we sing or, should I say, the lack of them. In regard to those we do sing, I am also concened, not because of their content so much as with the lack of it. For in leaving behind the hymns of previous centuries we have not only lost their rich theological content but a very powerful influence for good. Indeed, I believe that we have also robbed our souls of a rich ministry of truth, comfort and instruction.

For example, I cannot remember the last time I sang a hymn that reflects the spiritual warfare Christians are to wage against the enemy of their souls, such as 'Soldiers of Christ arise and put your armour on', 'Stand up, stand up for Jesus, you soldiers of the cross', 'Fight the good fight with all thy might', 'Who is on the Lord's side?' 'We rest on Thee our Shield and our Defender', 'Onward Christian soldiers, 'Christian, seek not yet repose; cast thy dreams of ease away; Thou art in the midst of foes: watch and pray.' Or the hymn of Isaac Watts written in the 17th Century, but one that continues to speak to the Church of our day,

> 'Are we the soldiers of the cross, the followers of the Lamb?
> And shall we fear to own His cause, or blush to speak His Name?

No! We must fight if we would reign: increase our courage, Lord;
We'll bear the toil, endure the pain, supported by Thy Word.'

Indeed, we seem, at times, to be living in an age of triumphalism; not that we are wrong to emphasise the victory that Christ has won for us, but let us never forget the words of the Saviour, that the devil goes around like a roaring lion (1 Peter Ch.5:8) seeking whom he may devour or like an angel of light (2 Corinthians Ch.11:14) seeking whom he may deceive. Let us remember the writings of John Bunyan; 'Pilgrims Progress' and, another of his books, 'The Holy War.'

I draw attention to this issue for one very important reason; it is my desire and intention, in what follows, to consider this whole subject of the Christian soldier and the Christian warfare as it is presented to us in the letter of the apostle Paul to the Ephesians, since I consider it to be a most critical issue, and yet one, I fear, that we do not take as seriously as we should. And so to begin with I would like to draw attention to this final chapter of his letter with special reference to the closing verses at the end of chapter six. For, as we can see from this short passage, it is in the form of an exhortation addressed not only to the Christians in the Church in Ephesus but to us all, to be good soldiers of the Lord Jesus Christ and to ensure that we are not only fully clothed in the armour which the Lord has furnished but that we are also equipped with the spiritual weapons which the Lord has provided.

However, in addressing this issue, it is not my intention to explore all the ramifications surrounding the Christian's struggle with sin and temptation or with the many problems we encounter in the living of the Christian life; not even with the work of evangelism in a hostile environment. The concern in these pages is with the subject which has been addressed by the Apostle Paul in this letter. The fact that what we consider here may have a relevance beyond the scope of our subject, while not intentional on my part, I trust may be welcome and helpful nonetheless.

The scriptures contain some thirteen epistles written by the Apostle Paul; fourteen, if we include the epistle to the Hebrews which, I am convinced, along with others, he wrote. Two epistles written by the Apostle Paul are of great importance, in that they both address the same issue, the issue of salvation. On the one hand we have his letter to the Christians in Rome. In this epistle the Apostle addresses himself to this great issue of salvation. And when we turn to his letter to the Ephesians we find him addressing the very same issue but with a very different purpose or concern. In his letter to the Christians in Rome we see that his concern is with 'how' the sinner is saved. In his letter to the Christians in Ephesus his concern is with 'why'.

In a consideration of the letter addressed to the Christians in Rome the Apostle begins by demonstrating the 'need' for salvation. We are sinners and, as such, we are cut off from God. Indeed we are living under the condemnation of His law. To make matters worse, we are not only incapable of saving ourselves, but due to the fact that we are spiritually dead in trespasses and sin, we are also unaware of our condition and quite unable, indeed, unwilling, to do anything about it. And so it is, the Lord in His wisdom gave us His law to instruct us as to our condition, and to reveal just how desperate our condition truly is. He then revealed the 'nature' of salvation in which he speaks of His marvelous plan of redemption. We are saved by grace through faith and that not of ourselves; it is the gift of God through the substitutionary death of the Lord Jesus Christ.

On turning to his letter to the Christians in Ephesus we soon discover that we have yet another letter which has, as its theme, the same issue of salvation. On this occasion, however, we see, in the opening chapter, that it has as its goal, not the 'how' of salvation, but the 'why'; the answer to which we find in the opening chapter and verses seven to ten, "In Him we have redemption through His blood, the forgiveness of sins, according to the riches of His grace which He made to abound towards us in all wisdom and prudence, having made known to us the mystery of His will, according to His good pleasure which He purposed in Himself, that in the dispensation of the fullness of the times <u>He might gather together in one all things in Christ, both which are in heaven and which are on earth – in Him.</u>"

This passage reveals the 'why' of salvation. With the entrance of sin certain consequences followed not least of which was a separating of God and man and an alienation of the man, (Adam) and his wife, (Eve) followed by the killing of their son by his brother. Satan's purpose and goal was not only to create division between the man and his Creator, but also to create enmity and division in the world of men. And from that fateful day the purpose of Satan has been to do just that, to disrupt, to divide and to destroy; to create a gulf, not only between God and man but between man and his fellowman.

In the Apostle's letter to the Romans we see God's plan to bring about reconciliation between man and his Creator. In this letter, we see God's purpose is to go further and reconcile, not only God and man, and man with his fellow man but 'all things in Christ, both which are in heaven and which are on earth.' Indeed, with this thought in mind we can approach this whole letter with a new understanding. This whole issue of reconciliation and unity dominates what the Apostle has written here in this epistle.

In his prayer in the opening chapter (verse 17f.) the apostle prays "that the God of our Lord Jesus Christ, the Father of glory, may give you the spirit of wisdom and revelation in the knowledge of Him, the eyes of your understanding being enlightened; that you may know what is the hope of His calling, what are the riches of the glory of His inheritance in the saints, and what is the exceeding greatness of His power toward us who believe, according to the working of His mighty power which He worked in Christ when He raised Him from the dead, and seated Him at His right hand in the heavenly places, far above all principality and power and might and dominion, and every name that is named, not only in this age but also in that which is to come. And He put all things under His feet, and gave Him to be head over all things to the church, which is His body, the fullness of Him who fills all in all."

In the second chapter, a chapter that is well known and well loved, the Apostle continues to use words such as 'we' and 'us' referring to the bringing together of both Jews and Gentiles stating in verse thirteen, "But now in Christ Jesus you who once were far off have been brought near by the blood of Christ. <u>For He Himself is our peace, Who has made both one, and has broken down the middle wall of separation…..so as to create in Himself one new man from the two, thus making peace, and that He might reconcile them both to God in one body, through the cross, thereby putting to death the enmity. And He came and preached peace to you who were afar off and to those who were near. For through Him we both have access by one Spirit to the Father. Now, therefore, you are no longer</u>

strangers and foreigners, but fellow citizens with the saints and members of the household of God, etc.

The third chapter continues this theme of the joining together of Jews and Gentiles in the body of Christ and of this being, "the mystery, which was from the beginning of the ages has been hidden in God Who created all things through Jesus Christ, to the intent that now the manifold wisdom of God might be made known by the church, etc." (Ch. 3:9-10).

In the fourth chapter also the apostle continues this theme with an exhortation in which the Apostle writes, "I, therefore, the prisoner of the Lord, beseech you to walk worthy of the calling with which you were called, with all lowliness and gentleness, with longsuffering, bearing with one another in love, endeavoring to keep the unity of the Spirit in the bond of peace. There is one body and one Spirit, just as you were called in one hope of your calling; one Lord, one faith, one baptism; one God and Father of all, Who is above all, and through all and in you all." (Ch. 4:1-6).

The Apostle then speaks of Christ equipping the church with "apostles, prophets, evangelists, pastors and teachers, for the equipping of the saints for the work of ministry, for the edifying of the Body of Christ, till we all come to the unity of the faith, etc." The Apostle continues in this vein throughout the rest of this chapter making yet another appeal in verse twenty five on the basis that, "we are members of one another."

In chapter five we have various exhortations to consider including his appeal to husbands and wives, leading into chapter six and the continued appeal to children and parents followed by yet another appeal to bondservants and to masters since it is within these close relationships that the issue of living together in peace and harmony is not only the most difficult challenge for us all but, where the issue of unity is most severely put to the test!

All of which brings us to the exhortation at the heart of this chapter if not the heart of this message to the Christians in Ephesus. As if to make this clear the Apostle begins this passage in verse ten with, "Finally, my brethren, be strong in the Lord and in the power of His might. Put on the whole armour of God that you may be able to stand against the wiles of the devil, etc."

We need to understand that when we come to these verses, the Apostle is not relinquishing his concern, he is not addressing a different issue; rather he has come to the very heart and climax of his message. From the fall of man in the garden of Eden to the end of his evil reign, Satan has had it as his goal to destroy all that God has created and in spite of the work of salvation he continues through his wicked wiles to cause as much chaos and suffering as he can for although he cannot undo what the Lord Jesus has done, he will do his level best to keep us all from enjoying the fruits of His salvation, or from manifesting them, whether the effect of Christ's reconciling us to God, or of His reconciling us to one another. The former is the concern of his letter to the Romans; the latter is the concern of his letter to the Ephesians.

In the book of Daniel we are given a rare insight into a realm that, even as committed Christians, we are inclined to overlook, ignore or even forget from time to time. Nevertheless, we cannot ever hope to understand the world we live in or the behavior of men apart from these insights furnished by the Word of God.

How often have we heard of some dreadful account of wickedness or act of violence and responded with a remark such as, 'How could anyone do such a thing?' 'How can any human being be so cruel or so heartless towards another human being?' And yet the world of men is far from being short of such examples for, as many tell us, 'we are not alone!' (Not that we believe in aliens so much as fallen angels.)

We may smile and shake our heads at such a comment, nevertheless, the fact is, what they are saying has more truth in it than anyone cares to admit. The bible has a number of accounts in which Satan is seen to be at work. The Lord Himself was tempted at the beginning of His ministry and all who seek to serve the Lord will face a similar adversary; and even if we are able to overcome in that hour of temptation, with the help of our Saviour, we will find that Satan will only 'leave us until a more convenient season.'

In coming back to the book of Daniel we find ourselves being taken behind the scenes. Here, we are permitted to observe and we are given a glimpse, of what is going on. We see just what it is that now controls, to some extent, the events that make up the story of man, both personally and universally. Indeed, as we see from this account, there is another realm, beyond our own, whose influence has a tremendous bearing upon the unfolding history of man, far more than you and I could ever imagine. I suggest that if we are to understand what the Apostle is saying at the end of this letter to the Church in Ephesus, we need to understand the significance of what we read in the book of Daniel. From what we read in the tenth chapter it would seem to be the case that angelic activity is very much behind the rise and decline of world powers but only as the Lord directs and controls.

Nor should we ever forget that it cost our Saviour dearly to purchase our pardon, to reconcile us to His Father and to one another. The fact is, the creating of this unity, bringing it into being, involved our Saviour in a dreadful struggle with this enemy of our souls as we see from His prayers in Gethsemane. Satan's power had to be broken that our souls might be set free. In the account of the Exodus we have a type, a picture, depicting this struggle to set God's people at liberty. The various plagues and the determined resistance of Pharoah to hold on to God's people only served to illustrate and foreshadow just how unwilling Satan would be to release God's people.

Maintaining this unity will also involve the people of God in a dreadful struggle as we see from the opening words of the Apostle in this tenth verse; "Finally, my brethren, be strong in the Lord and in the power of His might. Put on the whole armour of God that you may be able to stand against the wiles of the devil."

His first goal was to prevent the Lord from effecting His great work of reconciliation. In this attempt he failed. His goal now is to do all that he can to disrupt the relationship between the Lord and His people and between those who have been reconciled and their fellow Christians, their brothers and sisters in the Lord. However, although Satan appears to have created many divisions within the life of the Christian Church, the truth is, there has always been a genuine spirit of unity within the body of Christ. Unity does exist and will always exist in spite of all of his wiles and, wherever this spirit of fellowship and friendship is found, there we will find a true witness to the gospel. Indeed, the truth is that throughout the last 2000 years his attacks upon the Christian Church, whether doctrinally or through persecution, these attempts to divide us have only sent the Church back to their bibles or back into the arms of the Saviour. Indeed, the more Satan seeks to disturb our unity and divide us as God's people, the more the Lord employs these evil devices to purify the Church. With the rise of every falsehood and division within the Church, our Lord casts His people back upon their bibles only to expose what is false and to exalt what is true and with every wave of persecution He casts them, ultimately, upon Himself. Not that we can afford to be complacent here for the fact is, like the Children of Israel in the wilderness, we will pay a price for every mistake we make. Indeed, these verses contain what must be described as one of the clearest statements ever made on the nature of the Christian life; it is a warfare! A fierce battle from the day of our conversion to the day we enter into the presence of the Lord, an intense struggle and a battle which every Christian has to fight if we are to be faithful to our calling.

The point here being this; those of us who are genuine Christians and have accepted the Lord Jesus Christ as our Saviour, by virtue of our decision, soon discover that we have been plunged into a life of unavoidable and inevitable conflict, so much so, that I would be so bold as to say that anyone professing to be a follower of the Lord Jesus Christ who is not aware of any such conflict, is either failing to live as Christ would have them live (and is therefore being left alone by our enemy), or, is not truly converted at all since, from the moment we receive the Lord Jesus Christ as our Saviour and begin to live in obedience to the will of God, we will be brought into immediate conflict with Satan. No sooner was the Lord baptized than He was led into the wilderness to be tempted by the devil. Indeed, no one can understand the Christian life apart from this conflict. It is a spiritual conflict but one which is very real nonetheless and whether we like it or not, whether we recognise it or not, we are all involved and the question we need to be asking is put very well in the hymn written by Francis Ridley Havergal; having asked the question,

> "Who is on the Lord's side? Who will serve the King?" she goes on to say,
> "Fierce may be the conflict, strong may be the foe;
> But the King's own army none can overthrow.
> Round His standard ranging, victory is secure;
> For His truth unchanging makes the triumph sure.
> Joyfully enlisting, by Thy grace divine,
> We are on the Lord's side, Saviour, we are Thine.
> Chosen to be soldiers in an alien land,
> Chosen, called, and faithful for our Captain's band,
> In the service royal, let us not grow cold;
> Let us be right loyal, noble, true, and bold.
> Master, Thou wilt keep us, by Thy grace divine,
> Always on the Lord's side, Saviour, always Thine."

Having then considered the context of this appeal or exhortation, we now come to look more directly at these verses and their content beginning with the words at the beginning of this appeal, "Finally, my brethren,.." for this word, 'Finally' must not be misunderstood. It does not refer to the last in a series of instructions but rather to the climax of all that the Apostle has written thus far. There is a sense in which he has kept the most important command until the end. All that has gone before is important but this last word here is crucial. Like a wise parent instructing his children, the Apostle has kept the most important words of instruction to the last as if to say, whatever you do, take care to heed the words of instruction and advice that follow; "be strong in the Lord and in the power of His might. Put on the whole armour of God that you may be able to stand against the wiles of the devil." (Ch. 6:1f).

Until recent years many would have greeted such words of advice with a wry smile as belonging to another age where people were superstitious. Such words would have been considered as being out of place in our modern, scientific age. Today, however, these words are not out of place at all. Witchcraft and Satan worship are two of the fastest growing religions or cults in our western society. Indeed, I would be so bold as to say that there is no theme or subject that is more relevant to our understanding of the world around us at such a time as this. It not only provides us with the only adequate explanation of man's personal behavior but also provides us with an explanation and understanding of history and of the numerous forms of religion that bear witness to the religious consciousness in all of us and of our spiritual need. The realm we live in is not the only realm we need to consider when we think about mankind, the unfolding account of history or just try to understand the world around us.

Indeed, there is a very real sense in which what the Apostle says here is the most important part of this epistle for it is in this very passage that we see the cause of division between God and man and why the saving of our souls is such an onerous task requiring the eternal Son of God to lay aside His glory in order to suffer on the cross as a condemned criminal; and why it is that the saving of our souls is such a difficult task, and why, even after we are saved, we still have such a struggle throughout the course of our Christian lives.

Here, then, in these verses at the end of this epistle we have, not only the climax to the Apostle's message to the Church in Ephesus, but a message which was sent to the other Churches of his day and beyond, for the Apostle Paul was nearing the end of his life and was soon to be removed from this earthly scene. What he writes here is not only the climax of this letter but of his ministry. The point he is making before he departs is simply this, we are in a struggle, an important battle, from the moment we are saved. Like Israel in the wilderness there will be many who would seek to turn back rather than face the enemy. Nevertheless, if we are to enjoy the fruits of Christ's sacrifice we need to be willing to engage the enemy. For this we need faith and courage and, as Hebrews Ch.10:36 tells us, "you have need of endurance, so that after you have done the will of God, you may receive the promise." Let us listen then to these words of instruction from the Apostle Paul.

At the risk of laboring this issue may I suggest that we need to go back more often than we do to the story of Job. The lessons found within that important account of his awful sufferings and of the relationship and bearing that these two realms have upon one another, that is, the physical, material world and the spiritual, unseen world, have much to contribute to our understanding of ourselves and the world in which we live.

In looking at the attempt of Job's so-called friends to understand what was taking place, Job's response, the questions he asks, and the reaction of his wife, it becomes perfectly clear that nobody understood what was taking place until, that is, the Lord came upon the scene. Apart from that explanation we too would be in the dark as to what was going on in the life of Job at that time. Indeed, from this, we see how difficult, or should I say, impossible it is for us to make any real sense of the world we live in or of the events that make up the history of man. From the Word of God we deduce that a great deal, perhaps all, that takes place in the physical realm has as its source, as its cause, the influence, the effect of that struggle which is being waged in the spiritual realm between God and Satan. All of which brings us back to the writings of the Apostle Paul.

Why does he find it necessary to plead with God's people to maintain the unity of the Spirit in the bond of peace? Answer: because there is one who is committed to destroying that peace and to the setting of one Christian against another.

Why does he have so much to say on the need to know the truth? Answer: because there is one who perverts the truth and who would introduce doctrines of demons.

Why does he have so much to say about the maintaining of our Christian walk and the issue of morality? Answer: because there is one who would do all that he can to tempt us to go back to our sins once again.

Why does he have so much to say on the use of the tongue? Answer: because as James tells us the tongue is an unruly member which is set on fire by hell.

Why does he have so much to say about relationships? Answer: because he knows that there is one who is committed to the destroying of all relationships and who fosters selfishness and individualism, (the very issue the Apostle is addressing in this section of his letter).

Unfortunately, many Christians are not as aware of this conflict as they ought to be to the great cost of the Christian Church and their own blessing.

Chapter One: The Need To Be Strong

What the Apostle Paul does here is to address us with a very necessary word of admonition. Nor is that all he is doing, for in addition to this he has also provided us with a very necessary word of explanation in which we are given a most valuable insight into the whole nature of the Christian life, for what he tells us here is simply this, the Christian life is a spiritual warfare from which there is no escape until the day the Lord takes us to our eternal home; until then we will be engaged in this immense struggle against forces we cannot see and cannot defeat, by ourselves that is, which is why he exhorts us to 'be strong in the Lord and in the power of His might.' We cannot stand in our own strength and woe to those sheep that wander far from the protection of the Good Shepherd.

Therefore my first observation here would be this, with regard to this exhortation; being strong is our responsibility. The Apostle is clear about this as we can see from the fact that throughout this exhortation he addresses what he has to say, to us and to our responsibility; "be strong in the Lord" (verse 10), "Put on the whole armour of God," (verse 11) "Therefore take up the whole armour of God," (verse 13) "Stand therefore," (verse 14), "And take helmet of salvation and the sword of the Spirit." (verse 17). Nor is that all we derive from this passage. However, these are the most obvious and the most relevant examples. There are a number of other commands and exhortations implied in this passage. Nevertheless, from the above we may make a number of important observations and deductions.

[1.] It Is Possible To Be A Christian And Yet To Be Weak:

It is possible to be saved and yet to have no strength spiritually. Like the disciples before the death and resurrection of the Lord who, although they were true believers, were, nevertheless, men of little faith unable as yet to understand what the Lord was doing or where the Lord was going. They had little confidence in His wisdom or in His judgment. As in the storm on the lake of Galilee they were fearful and prone to panic when events took a turn which they did not understand. As yet they were unprepared for the hour of trial that was about to come upon them to test them. Thus, when the enemy finally came to arrest the Lord the disciples fled. This is what happens when our faith is weak and we fail to be strong in the Lord. Few Christians will be a stranger to such times in their experience and so we fail to stand!

[2.] It Is The Christian's Responsibility To Ensure That They Are Strong:

This we see from this passage as the various exhortations make abundantly clear. Indeed, the very fact that the apostle addresses us in this way indicates that the answer to our state of weakness lies with us. We are responsible for our own condition. Physical strength comes through exercise and spiritual strength comes in a similar way. We must study to show ourselves approved unto God. Indeed, as physical strength is the result of regular exercise, spiritual strength requires no less a commitment.

Under great pressure, the Hebrew Christians were sorely tempted to go back to Judaism. It was a dreadful trial, and their faith was being put through a very severe test to the point where the writer had to warn them in no uncertain terms that to fail now would destroy their witness and even put their souls in great danger. And so it is he exhorts them, "Therefore do not cast away your confidence, which has great reward. For you have need of endurance, so that after you have done the will of God, you may receive the promise, 'For yet a little while, and He Who is coming will come and shall not tarry. Now the just shall live by faith; but if anyone draws back, My soul has no pleasure in him.' But we are not of those who draw back to perdition, but of those who believe to the saving of the soul." (Hebrews Ch.10:35–39).

In the scriptures the Christian is described as a living stone, not as a jelly that takes on the form of the dish into which it is poured; which brings us to consider the third point here.

[3.] Strength Is Needed If We Are To Live The Christian Life:

For as we see from this passage and others within the Word of God, the acquiring of strength is both commended and commanded implying that it is essential to the living of the Christian life. It is not acquired quickly or easily as we have noted above and spiritual strength, like physical strength is also hard to acquire but easily lost.

Many years ago I preached a series of sermons on the names or titles used by the Lord to reveal Himself to His people. I was interested in one particular title given first of all to Abram in Genesis where He reaffirms His covenant with him (Ch. 17:1); "When Abram was ninety-nine years old, the Lord appeared to Abram and said to him, "I (am) Almighty God; walk before Me and be blameless."

The title used here, and in a number of other passages, is, in the Hebrew, El Shaddai, (El being the name for God and Shaddai being a plural word, the singular of which is 'shad', the word for the breast on which the newborn child is weaned. And although some

Hebrew scholars hesitate in regard to this translation since the word is used for the male as well as the female, I much prefer this meaning to the other since it carries with it the notion, not of the chest muscles of the man (since the strength of the man is more appropriately portrayed in the strong 'arm' of the man) but of that strength imparted directly from a mother to the newborn child which in turn implies that our 'being strong in the Lord' is not so much a strength exercised on our behalf as a strength imparted to each of His children directly by the Lord Himself as we feed upon the milk of His word.

Chapter Two: The Nature Of Our Strength

In his letter to the Hebrews the apostle makes it clear that although at the beginning of our Christian lives we begin with the milk of the word we are not expected to remain on that level. As he tells them, "He became the author of eternal salvation to all who obey Him, called by God as High Priest 'according to the order of Melchizedek,' of whom we have much to say, and hard to explain, since you have become dull of hearing. For though by this time you ought to be teachers, you need someone to teach you again the first principles of the oracles of God; and you have come to need milk and not solid food. For everyone who partakes only of milk is unskilled in the word of righteousness, for he is a babe. But solid food belongs to those who are of full age, that is, those who by reason of use have their senses exercised to discern both good and evil." (Hebrews Ch.5:10-14).

Now, although we are dealing here essentially with the issue of spiritual strength, we may find a number of important lessons by comparing this realm with the natural realm. To be strong physically requires commitment, a fairly strict and healthy diet, regular exercise and proper times of rest among other things. In preparing ourselves for this spiritual warfare we need to take great care not to be found unfit or unprepared. And so it is, we need to give our close attention to the exhortation of the Apostle in these closing verses of this epistle, remembering, of course that what the Apostle is concerned with in these verses is only one aspect of this conflict, the issue of maintaining that Christian unity which the Lord Jesus died to secure within the body of Christ.

As we have seen, the above has been the concern of the Apostle Paul throughout this letter; not the creating of this unity, but the preserving of that unity which Christ has already created through His death on the cross and a work of grace in the lives of His people, a unity He had already prayed for on a previous occasion (as we see from John Ch:17:11, 20 – 21). All through this epistle the Apostle Paul has been addressing this issue as we saw in an earlier chapter. It is imperative therefore that we take seriously this exhortation here in regard to the enemy of our souls. Spiritual warfare is real, as is our enemy. We may not see him but we can be sure that he is committed to the dividing of God's people and will stop at nothing to destroy what Christ has created. Where he sows discord, the witness of the Church to the Lord and to the gospel will be compromised and undermined. He cannot destroy this unity but he can keep it from being expressed (to others) and enjoyed (by ourselves). Let us recognise that behind every breakdown in our relationships we will find the hand of our enemy is at work. What then can we do about it? The Apostle has some good advice in what follows.

As any faithful student of the scriptures recognises, the words of the Apostle Paul are always very carefully chosen and so it is somewhat significant that in the words before us, we have a sentence which may be taken as a word of advice, as a word of instruction, or even as a word of command. Now in one sense, they are all of these. However, the more important question is, what does he mean by this? After all, if the responsibility to "be strong" is ours, does that mean that the strength is ours also? Are we capable of producing such strength by ourselves?

Fortunately, to keep us from going astray in our thinking on this issue the apostle provides the answer in this very same verse.

We are to "be strong in the Lord and in the power of His might." Our strength is a derived strength; derived from outside of ourselves. God Himself is the source of our strength. He is El Shaddai, the Almighty, dispensing strength to His people as we have already seen. We are to be strong in the Lord and in the power of His might by feeding upon the milk of His word. Herein we find the source of our strength. The Lord does not, in this case at least, act on our behalf, but rather, He is the One who provides us with the strength and nourishment in order to enable us to take a stand against an enemy who is stronger than we are. No Christian has the power or the strength to live the Christian life on their own any more than they have the ability or power to save themselves. We are as dependent upon the Lord for the one as for the other. Nor is our strength to be found in that which is natural but in that which is spiritual. Our greatest need is to look to the Lord and to trust in Him by faith.

However, right here is where we find our greatest problem. When we encounter an issue, a need, a situation or difficulty we cannot see any answer to, we tend to question the Lord like the children of Israel in the wilderness whenever they met with a need or encountered a problem for which they could see no solution or find any answer to.

Nor is this a new dilemma as we see only too well from the number of examples that we find in the scriptures such as Abram and Sarah being told that they would be parents when Sarah was past the age of child bearing; or the children of Israel at the Red Sea with nowhere to go and the approach behind them of the Egyptian army. Examples could be multiplied by those of us who have been Christians for any length of time. Indeed, we can probably testify to the Lord's timely interventions in our own lives on occasions when we could see no solutions or answers to the problems we were facing. Faith is a constant and very necessary requirement.

Another important observation we need to make as we begin to look at this exhortation is that it is addressed to every Christian and not just to the leadership of the Church. The leadership of the Church play a vital role in this warfare it is true. However, we do not set them aside in order to fight this war on our behalf. We must engage in this battle ourselves. We too must take these words to heart. In fact, there is probably no passage of scripture that has been more important or more relevant to the unfolding story of the Christian Church and its witness than this one. Furthermore, I am utterly convinced that our welfare, our spiritual well being and our future as the Christian Church will be determined by our response to this appeal by the Apostle. For here in these verses he is giving to these early Christians some of the most important words of instruction he ever gave to the Church of Jesus Christ. Nor is that all, for the Apostle included a number of reasons as to why they are to take these instructions seriously.

In telling them what to do he also tells them why they need to do it; "that you may be able to stand against the wiles of the devil. For we do not wrestle against flesh and blood, but against principalities, against powers, against the rulers of the darkness of this age, against spiritual hosts of wickedness in the heavenly places." (vrs. 11-12). The Apostle knows only too well what is at stake here, the credibility of our message and the witness of the Christian Church to the world we live in. Indeed, in the course of his own ministry he had encountered a great deal of opposition to his message both from the heathen idolaters of his day as well as from those of the circumcision party, not to mention the heretical teachers within the

Church itself at whose hands he had suffered great physical persecution and abuse.

When we turn to the letter to the Hebrews we see what can happen under a prolonged period of opposition and suffering. We might begin well as those early Christians had. Nevertheless, the Apostle is at great pains to strengthen their faith by holding the Lord Jesus up before them, referring also to the faithful witness of those who had gone before them in spite of all that they had been called upon to endure appealing to them throughout this letter not to give way to the pressure of persecution and reminding them of their initial response to the gospel; "But recall the former days in which, after you were illuminated, you endured a great struggle with sufferings: partly while you were made a spectacle both by reproaches and tribulations, and partly while you became companions of those who were so treated; for you had compassion on me in my chains, and joyfully accepted the plundering of your goods, knowing that you have a better and an enduring possession for yourselves in heaven. Therefore do not cast away your confidence which has great reward. <u>For you have need of endurance, so that after you have done the will of God, you may receive the promise:</u> 'For yet a little while, and He who is coming will come and will not tarry'" for, "we are not of those who draw back to perdition, but of those who believe to the saving of the soul." (Hebrews Ch. 11:32-39).

The apostle is only too aware as to what is at stake here; without this the Christian Church will lose its credibility and its witness, our preaching will be empty, the souls of men will remain unmoved and unchanged, the Lord will not be glorified, Christ will not be exalted, our hypocrisy will be evident to all, we will not be the witness to the power of the gospel as we were intended to be and we will be unable to stand, either because we are unwilling to do so or because we are unable to do so. This then is the Apostles great concern for us all; are we able to stand? Can we take the pressure? Like many since, they were prepared for some opposition and they had begun well but were quite unprepared for the continuing stress and strain that they were now being called upon to endure. Some were clearly beginning to lose heart and even to lose hope; a situation which is hardly unique to the early Christian Church. After all we are living in a world today where the god of this world is seeking to utterly depose the Lord and to hinder His great purpose to redeem it and to repossess it. These words of the Apostle are as relevant today as when they were first written; "Finally my brethren, be strong in the Lord and in the power of His might. Put on the whole armour of God that you may be able to stand against the wiles of the devil"; an appeal which is not only suited to the end of this letter but one which, in a very real sense is appropriate and suited to be placed at the end of every letter in the New Testament. Indeed, there is perhaps no passage of scripture which is more relevant to the Christian church today than this one. We are to stand in the face of temptation, opposition, the many pressures to compromise, persecution, and, as the apostle says, the very wiles of the devil. This we cannot do in our own strength. We could more easily stand on the exposed roof of a high building in the teeth of a hurricane and defy the wind than stand against the wiles of the devil in our own strength without the Lord.

Chapter Three: The Wiles of The Devil

Following the two world wars which were fought during the first half of the twentieth century, and perhaps as a reaction to the horrors experienced and witnessed by so many during those years, we entered an age of materialism and scientific advance where we saw the Churches, which, during these conflicts, people had frequented in order to pray for their loved ones, beginning to empty. Of course, the previous century had made its own contribution to this trend through the rise of rationalism and the theory of evolution. However, that is not the problem today. Indeed, it is quite the opposite. The age of materialism proved to be full of promises it could never fulfill. It only proved to be a false hope. Materialism, so far from satisfying the deeply felt needs of mankind was very quickly seen to be an utter delusion for it only served to give rise to an even greater and deeper sense of need. Like many cultures before them, the more wealth people accumulated, the more possessions they acquired, the more miserable they became and the more empty they felt their lives to be. In desperation many of the younger generation, and others who were not so young, found themselves turning to all kinds of drugs and hedonistic pleasures to fill the emptiness. This, sad to say, only made matters worse and merely revealed just how desperate our modern society had become.

In recent years our western society, it seems, has come full circle and the rising interest in witchcraft and Satan worship is seen to be increasing at a tremendous rate. Nor is it limited to the poor and ignorant in our society but is very much the domain of the wealthy intellectuals of our western world. Meanwhile, we see the strange silence of the Christian Churches in our day on this issue. We are still living in the shadow of the nineteenth century and the effect of evolutionary thinking, the age of rationalism, liberalism and of the so called intellectualism of that period. Indeed, a great deal of money, time and effort has gone into making the Church 'more seeker friendly, more approachable, more entertaining and enjoyable' not to mention more 'useful, more helpful in the community'. We are more socially aware than we have ever been. However, I do believe that we have paid an awful price for this ecclesiastical facelift. We are now afraid to speak about sin and the need for repentance. This presents quite a contrast to the first public appearance of the Lord Jesus Christ as we see from the account in the gospel of Mark. Preceded by John the Baptist who, we are told in the opening chapter of this gospel, "came baptizing in the wilderness and preaching a baptism of repentance for the remission of sins", we read in that same chapter, following the imprisonment of John, that "Jesus came to Galilee, preaching the gospel of the kingdom of God, and saying, 'The time is fulfilled, and the kingdom of God is at hand. Repent and believe in the gospel.'" This too is where we need to begin with our message. It is not directed primarily on the intellectual level but on the spiritual level. As the Apostle tells us in his first letter to the Corinthians, "For the message of the cross is foolishness to those who are perishing, but to us who are being saved it is the power of God. For it is written: 'I will destroy the wisdom of the wise, and bring to nothing the understanding of the prudent.' Where is the wise? Where is the scribe? Where is the disputer of this age? Has not God made foolish the wisdom of this world? For since in the wisdom of God, the world through wisdom did not know God, it pleased God through the foolishness of the message preached to save those who believe." (Ch. 1:18 – 21).

Indeed, in the very next chapter we have another reminder, if we needed one that is, of the spiritual nature of gospel preaching. In this chapter we read of spiritual wisdom. And having described how this spiritual wisdom has been given to us the Apostle went on to say, "These things we also speak, not in words which man's wisdom teaches but which the Holy Spirit teaches, comparing spiritual things with spiritual. But the natural man does not receive the things of the Spirit of God, for they are foolishness to him; nor can he know them, because they are spiritually discerned." (1 Cor. Ch.2:13-14). And so it is, our task is not to try and make our message more intellectually acceptable, nor more palatable, nor more 'seeker friendly' and appealing. We are to declare the truth as it is in God's word and look to the Lord to bless it to the saving of precious souls for whom Christ died. To ignore the spiritual nature of our message and our task, is to fail to get our message across and is to fail in our God given mission. For this reason, and for this reason only, we may welcome the renewed interest in the spiritual realm.

Having established the spiritual nature of this conflict, the next order of business must be to consider just who we are fighting. Who is our enemy and why is he being so aggressive towards us? What is his objective? What is his goal? What kind of army does he have, what kind of weapons does he possess and what tactics will he employ against us? These are just some of the questions we need to be asking before we rush off into battle or even begin to put our armour on.   In answer to this the Apostle tells us that we need to be strong in the Lord and in the power of His might. We are to put on the whole armour of God in order that we may be able to stand against the wiles of the devil. The question then is this, what are the wiles of the devil? What exactly does this statement refer to? And how can we overcome them? How can we defeat him? And so it is the Apostle tells us about our adversary and then, following that, he describes in some detail something of the Christians armoury.

1. The Christian's Adversary Explained

It would seem to be a stating of the obvious to say that any soldier going into battle would be very unhappy to say the least if he knew nothing at all about the enemy, who they were, how he would recognise them, what kind of weapons they possessed, the kind of tactics they would employ, etc. Such information is invaluable in preparing to engage any antagonist.

In the realm of sport or in any form of competition it would be very foolish not to study your opponent, his strengths and his weaknesses, etc. for this will be very helpful in seeking to anticipate their movements and to interpret their activities and so, in the light of the fact that our problems began in the garden of Eden, it is to that event, first of all, that we must turn in order to see what lessons we can learn from what happened there.

Before we do, however, perhaps we should make reference to yet one other valuable lesson we can learn from the realm of sport; one which has particular reference to those team sports which require a number of highly trained and highly skilled players possessing a variety of skills required for their particular event. Not only must they ever be conscious of the goal and the objective of their particular sport, but they should also be aware of the skills and positions of their team-mates. There are lessons here for us all to learn! Let us ever recall the very sad story of Laish! (Judges Ch.18:7).

Looking more directly now at our enemy, we can see from the record we have in Genesis chapter three, that the Lord provides us with a very important insight into the character and conduct we can expect to encounter in our dealings with Satan.

To begin with we see that his first move is to come to Eve and not to Adam in order to sow seeds of doubt in her mind concerning what God had said, and this approach is very interesting for a number of reasons. In the first place we see that he does not contradict the Lord to His face. Satan is too subtle for that. Nor does he come to Eve when Adam is around. Instead, he waits until Eve is by herself. And how often have we seen this evil tactic employed by those who follow his example. How many people have we known who, in seeking to destroy our relationships with others, have employed this tactic to sow seeds of doubt and suspicion as to our character, our motives and our genuine friendship with the person they are talking to in order to undermine that friendship to their own advantage. How many relationships have been damaged or destroyed in this way never again to be repaired or restored. This is just a part of his wicked legacy. Satan was the very first gossip! As the Lord said 'Satan was a liar and the father of lies' from the beginning (John Ch.8:44).

Secondly, we see that Satan not only fails to say anything when the Lord is present (or at least is manifestly present) nor does he say anything when Adam is around. Instead, He begins his wicked insinuations with Eve when she is by herself. After all, he knows that Adam is far more likely to listen to his wife than he is to listen to the serpent. He loves his wife and, for that reason, is far more vulnerable when, having taken of the forbidden fruit, she now seeks to persuade her husband to eat of it. After all, she had tasted of the fruit and had not died. Perhaps Satan was telling the truth when he said you will not surely die. The fact is, however, the covenant had been made with Adam and not with Adam and Eve. And so, it was only when Adam ate of the fruit that we are told that the eyes of both of them were opened and only at that point were they seen to be naked.

As to what the devil was implying in his conversation with Eve, it appears to be obvious from the words he employed that he was suggesting, or insinuating, that God was being less than honest with them. He begins with the question, "Has God said?" only to then openly contradict God's words with "you shall not die"; a contradiction and a downright lie. Nor have these tactics ever changed. He still seeks to sow seeds of doubt in the minds of men with regard to the character of God and of His word. He would have us believe that neither God nor His word can be trusted and that He is withholding something from us which would be to our advantage. And this is a tactic Satan has employed throughout history as we see both under the Old Testament and under the New. Like Achan (Joshua Ch. 7:1f) at the fall of Jericho, seeing the spoils of war which God had forbidden, he thought that the Lord was being unfair to forbid them to take anything for themselves, only to perish for his disobedience along with his family; as was the case with Adam and his family (or posterity).

So it has been down through the ages. Satan has sought to oppose God's word. He will do all that he can to contradict it, deny it and even remove it from God's people as he did in the days of the kings of Israel and Judah as we learn from the historical record under the Old Testament. Rediscovered in the days of Josiah the reading of it led to conviction, fear, repentance and reformation as was the case during the religious Reformation in the middle ages. Indeed, following the time of the Apostles and even before the end of the apostolic period, we see that there were many who sought to deny and undermine its' teaching and although the Lord preserved the truth in a number of ways and in a number of places, the fact is that to a large extent the truth was hidden for many years until the time of the Reformation. As the Lord taught us in the parable of the sower with regard to the seed that was sown on the path, a path which had become hardened by the feet of men walking on it, when the seed is sown upon the hardened ground, the birds of the air will come and take it away.

Another observation we can make here is in regard to the warning of God should Adam be tempted to disobey Gods' command. Before Eve was created Adam was told, "Of every tree of the garden you may freely eat; but of the tree of the knowledge of good and evil you shall not eat, for in the day you eat of it you shall surely die." To this warning Satan responded by saying to the woman, "You will not surely die." Since then, man has been defiant, refusing to take this threat seriously. This was the case in the days of Noah and throughout the history of Israel during the Old Testament. It will be the case in the end time as the Apostle Peter tells us in his second letter and in the third chapter. Liberal theology has sought to deny that a day of judgement is coming or that when sinners die they go to hell to await that dreadful day when the Lord will judge the world in righteousness. The devil is still whispering in the ears of sinners, "You will not surely die." This is a teaching that has had a marked influence upon the Christian Churches of our day. God is a God of love, we are told, and therefore the belief that He will send anyone to hell for eternity must be wrong. We are to love Him, not fear Him, a view that has had a marked impact upon the preaching of the gospel in our day. And so it is, as the psalmist tells us in Psalm

36:1 regarding those who are 'wicked', "There is no fear of God before his eyes"; and in Psalm 111:10 we have another important statement regarding the need to fear the Lord, "The fear of the Lord is the beginning of wisdom."

The whole purpose and aim of the devil is to convince us all, that Gods' word cannot be trusted on the basis that he, the devil, tells us so, and thus he would shift the seat of authority from what God says to what he says.

Without the fear of the Lord the end result is that chaos, confusion, anarchy, rebellion and unrestrained sin have been introduced into the world of men and the wiles of the devil have varied little since then.

Nor is that all we learn from this encounter with Eve as another important observation might be made here with regard to the timing of this attack. Satan makes his move right at the very beginning when neither Adam nor Eve had been given the chance to taste of Gods' goodness. So too at the time of our Saviours birth. Through Herod Satan sought to destroy the young Child. And many a convert can testify to the difficulties they encountered at the time of their conversion. The angels in heaven may rejoice when a sinner is converted but the exact opposite is true of the demons in hell! They rage! Nevertheless, as our heavenly Father cared for His young Son then, so too He cares for His own today and we all owe more than we realise to the providence and protecting hand of God with regard to those early days in our Christian life.

How lacking in wisdom is a child; how quick to believe all that they are told; how innocent and unsuspecting are they; how weak and helpless; how lacking in knowledge; how willing to accept everything at face value; and how easily led astray are they! It is a wonder that we make it through those early years to adulthood. Nor is our spiritual childhood very different. The Lord indeed is very gracious!

Another occasion which the devil employs to attack us is when we are low spiritually or physically (or both) during times of suffering, weakness, weariness or in a time of trials where we encounter problems or difficulties which threaten to overwhelm us. At such times he will seize the opportunity to tempt us to question the Lord and His goodness.

The Lord knows our frame; He remembers that we are dust (Psalm 103:14). So, too, does Satan! He knows that there are limits to our endurance and limits to our strength. As an experienced general laying siege to a city, he watches for an area of weakness or a momentary lapse on the part of the citizens; for a weak spot on the walls where he can launch his attack using his most experienced troops at a time chosen by him in order to conquer his enemy in one swift action which will provide him with a quick victory rather than have his army endure a long protracted campaign. Jobs' wife sought to persuade him that he should curse God and die. Even the Lord Jesus was tempted by the devil in the wilderness after He had fasted for forty days and was hungry.

A third occasion during which we find Satan attacking God's people is at the commencement of some great work for God; an example of which is found in the story of the returning exiles, first under Ezra and then under Nehemiah, in regard to the rebuilding of the Temple followed some years later on by the rebuilding of the walls of Jerusalem. On both occasions the people of God were opposed by their enemies. Indeed, returning again to the account of the Lords' baptism prior to the beginning of His ministry, we see Him being led by the Spirit into the wilderness to be tempted by the devil. Another example being that of the Apostle Paul having to leave Damascus at night by a basket lowered over the city walls in order to escape from those who were determined to put an end to his ministry before he had even begun. And may we never forget Gethsemane!

Another occasion Satan often employs is when we are not where we should be and are found looking upon that which is forbidden as Eve, for example, looking upon the fruit or as Achan who confessed, "When I saw among the spoils, a beautiful Babylonian garment, two hundred shekels of silver, and a wedge of gold weighing fifty shekels, I coveted them and took them." (Joshua Ch. 7:20-21). Even king David, we are told, at a time when kings go forth to war, was found at home, on the roof of his house when he happened to see Bathsheba. Like many others, he looked upon that which was forbidden and took it for himself. As the words of the chorus tell us, 'Be careful little eyes what you see.'

Fifthly, and finally, our old age, as we get near to the finish line, is another occasion when we may be prone to the attacks of the devil. Moses struck the rock in anger; Isaacs' eyes grew dim, a condition that was indicative of his spiritual blindness in regard to the Lords' will for his two sons. He had a favourite son, Esau, due to his ability as a hunter as opposed to Jacobs' position in the home as the favourite of his mother; King David numbered the people and King Solomon had his head turned by his many wives and concubines in spite of the fact that he was the wisest man who ever lived.

Perhaps we ought to include another observation here regarding the call of the Lord to the ministry or to the mission field since it would not be the first time that a Christian was persuaded not to follow their conviction due to the appeal, or the pressure of those nearest to them, not to go. As with the Lord Jesus, Satan would have us fall down before him and, just as he offered to give our Saviour the kingdoms of this world should He choose to do so, he will be pleased to give us what we desire. Of course to do so would avoid the way of the cross and leave the devil to be the ruler of this world. The apostle Peter too, out of love for the Lord also sought to have Him avoid the way of the cross for which he received a stern response from the Saviour, Who, recognizing the true source of this appeal replied, 'Get behind Me, Satan! You are an offense to Me, for you are not mindful of the things of God, but the things of men.' (Matt.Ch.16:23). Indeed, this sounds a warning to us all. Whether we are seeking advice or are in the business of offering advice, we need to be careful. The less painful path may not be the path of obedience; the less difficult path may not be the path of blessing; on the other hand, the hardest road may not be the road to victory.

These, then, are just some of the occasions when we should be alert and upon our guard against Satan's devices.

Having looked briefly then at the Christians' Adversary, we move on now to look in a more positive note at our own resources.

2. The Christians Armoury Expounded

Having considered who our enemy is and what his goal is and how he seeks to achieve it, we now need to look more closely at our own resources. We are now aware of the devils tactics or, as the Apostle describes them, 'the wiles of the devil', and so, like the young servant of Elisha we need to look up from the enemies gathered around us in order to see the bigger picture and the unseen armies of the Lord surrounding us above, prepared and ready to both defend us and deliver us. We also need to consider the provision the Lord has made for our defense; the Christian's armour.

In preparation for any kind of warfare it is absolutely necessary to study the nature of our enemies, their numbers, their tactics, their weapons, their experience, their objectives, etc. However, it is just as important to consider, at the same time, our own potential; our numbers, our tactics, our weapons, our experience, our goals and objectives, our own potential and our leader, our captain, our general. After all, any leader who only studies his enemy and fails to take stock of his own resources is not worthy to be in a position of leadership. He must be well acquainted with both.

In the passage before us we find references to both. On the one hand we are exhorted to be strong in the Lord and in the power of His might and, at the same time, to put on the whole armour of God in order that we may be able to be able to stand against the wiles of the devil.

It is so important in coming to these few verses that we constantly bear in mind that they are not referring to the task of evangelism where the Christian is called upon to go into all the world to make disciples; to lay siege to the unbelieving world; that world which lies in the grasp of the devil. The concern in this passage is exactly the same concern we have seen expressed and addressed throughout this entire epistle; the spiritual unity of those who have been reconciled both to God and to their fellow Christians. Thus, the exhortation is to "be strong in the Lord and in the power of His might. Put on the whole armour of God that you may be able to stand against the wiles of the devil." This passage is primarily concerned with the 'preserving of the unity of the Spirit in the bond of peace.' (Eph. Ch.4:3). The desire of the Apostle here then is that we may, having availed ourselves of this armour, be able to stand against the wiles of the devil whose primary goal and objective is to produce division and to promote the destruction of all relationships both between God and man and between man and his fellow man with special concern for those who have been saved and thus have been reconciled both to the Lord and to one another. This, Satan would undo if he could.

It must also be recognised, therefore, that we are not being exhorted or commanded here to do all that we can to create this unity. What the Apostle is exhorting us to do is to ensure that we preserve that unity and protect that unity against the attacks of the devil and those demonic spirits under his control. This is our position; this is our condition, and one we need to be properly equipped to preserve. Indeed, two things need to be said here both of which are important. On the one hand we are to be suitably attired in the armour that God has provided, for that is our responsibility and one we need to take very seriously. And, secondly, we need to stand our ground, we need to take the place which the Lord has assigned to us in order that we may guard it; to keep the enemy from creating a place of weakness in our ranks.

It is important, therefore, in seeking to consider the nature of our armour and our weapons, that we take note of what the Apostle tells us in that very important statement which we find in the Apostles' second letter to the Christians in Corinth (Ch.10:3-4) where he enlightens us with regard to the very nature of this conflict, "For though we walk in the flesh, we do not war according to the flesh. For the weapons of our warfare are not carnal but mighty in God for the pulling down of strongholds."

It is important therefore to realise that the armor we are given and the weapons the Lord makes available to us, are suited to the spiritual nature of this warfare and that we are personally responsible for appropriating and employing them, for, as the Apostle tells us in Ephesians Chapter 6:13, 'Therefore, <u>take up</u>' (and right here we see where the responsibility lies. <u>We</u> are commanded to take up) 'the whole armor of God, that you may be able to withstand in the evil day, and having done all, to stand'. For, without this armor and without these weapons, we will find it impossible to stand our ground; we will find it impossible to remain faithful. For it is right here that we find the key to the whole issue of this spiritual warfare. "Having done all, to stand!" For more than once Gods' people were told to stand still and see the salvation of the Lord: on one occasion by the Red Sea (Exodus Ch.14:13); and, on another occasion, when the combined forces of the Moabites, Ammonites and others came against King Jehoshaphat and the people with him while they were outnumbered and afraid. A Levite, Jahaziel by name, addressed the King and those with him, saying, "Listen, all you of Judah and you inhabitants of Jerusalem, and you, King Jehoshaphat! Thus says the Lord to you: 'Do not be afraid or dismayed because of this great multitude, for the battle is not yours, but God's. You will not need to fight in this battle. Position yourselves, stand still and see the salvation of the Lord.'" (2 Chron. Ch.20:15-17). This account is as worthy of our consideration as it is suited to our encouragement.

The following are also found to be addressing this whole issue and therefore are also worthy of our attention; "Therefore, my beloved brethren, be steadfast, immovable, always abounding in the work of the Lord, knowing that your labor is not in vain in the Lord." (1 Corinthians Ch. 15:58); "Watch, stand fast in the faith, be brave, be strong." (1 Corinthians Ch. 16:13); "Stand fast therefore in the liberty by which Christ has made us free, etc." (Galatians Ch.5:1); "Therefore submit to God. Resist the devil and he will flee from you." (James Ch. 4:7); "Be sober, be vigilant; because your adversary walks about like a roaring lion, seeking whom he may devour. Resist him, steadfast in the faith, etc." (1 Peter Ch. 5:8-9); "Only let your conduct be worthy of the gospel of Christ, so that whether I come and see you or am absent, I may hear of your affairs, that you stand fast in one spirit, with one mind, striving together for the faith of the gospel."(Philippians Ch.1:27); and "Therefore, my beloved and longed-for brethren, my joy and crown, so stand fast in the Lord, beloved."(Philippians Ch. 4:1).

Chapter Four: For We Wrestle

The issue before us is much more than an academic issue. It has a very practical bearing on our Christian lives as we see from the letter to the Hebrews. Having come to the Lord through the preaching of those early apostles and evangelists they would have been aware that, more than likely, they would meet with opposition and even persecution, either from the Jewish community, or from the pagan world. However, as time passed and the persecution continued, some had begun to waver, so much so, that the author wrote this letter to warn them of the danger they would face should they be tempted to return to Judaism; "But recall the former days in which, after you were illuminated, you endured a great struggle with sufferings: partly while you were made a spectacle both by reproaches and tribulations, and partly while you became companions of those who were so treated; for you had compassion on me in my chains, and joyfully accepted the plundering of your goods, knowing that you had a better and an enduring possession for yourselves in heaven. Therefore do not cast away your confidence, which has great reward. For you have need of endurance, so that after you have done the will of God, you may receive the promise." (Ch 10:32-36).

In the parable of the sower the Lord warned us of the danger of being shallow ground as the seed sown would not be able to find enough depth of soil in order to send down roots deep enough to survive the heat of the sun when it rose to warm the ground. And the sad fact is men have often been guilty of not being thorough in their thinking whether in matters scientific or in matters spiritual and the results have often been critical resulting in serious losses. In coming to the Lord as our Saviour we have often failed to count the cost in spite of the teaching of the Lord on this whole issue of discipleship. We are to be willing to take up our own cross in order to follow Him. We are entering a spiritual warfare and need to be willing to take up our spiritual armour in order that we may be able to stand. Becoming a Christian may seem, in the thinking of some, to be nothing more than a simple matter of believing the message of the gospel. Belonging to Christ, however, requires each believer to take their stand in the ranks of those who have also come to believe in Him. We are not only saved from our sin, we are also saved to serve; we are His servants, we are His soldiers, called to take our stand against a very powerful enemy. This is not some intellectual issue for us to debate or discuss but a very serious and practical matter affecting us all.

In the Old Testament scriptures we find that there are a number of types and pictures which the Holy Spirit employs to depict the Person of the Lord Jesus Christ and the great work of salvation and deliverance He comes to perform. He is the fulfillment of many types and offices; in the Tabernacle and later Temple He is represented by the Ark of the covenant, the veil of the Temple, the showbread, the High Priest, the sacrificial animals and birds, the golden altar, to name but a few; He is *the* Prophet, Priest and King, the chief cornerstone, the rock that, being struck in the wilderness produced the water of life for God's people, the manna and a multitude of other types and pictures. And so it is here in the picture of the Christian warfare. On the one hand the Christian sees his role as a soldier taking his place in the ranks and on the other as a wrestler in a struggle with a much stronger foe which is why the Apostle exhorts us to "be strong in the Lord and in the power of His might." (Vrs. 10).

Thus, on the one hand we have a picture of the Christian soldier dressed in full battle armour needing to hold out against the devil and his evil servants whilst on the other hand we read in verse twelve of this sixth chapter, "For we do not wrestle against flesh and blood, but against principalities, against powers, against the rulers of the darkness of this age, against spiritual hosts of wickedness in the heavenly places", a rather different picture to that of the Christian soldier in full battle armour. Nor is the Apostle mixed up in his illustrations here for both of these pictures are valid and both need to be employed to provide us with a true picture of the Christian warfare.

Clearly, we do not put armour on to wrestle nor are we contending with flesh and blood, a human foe. This is a spiritual wrestling match with spiritual foes who are stronger than we are. This issue is a serious one but one which we are helped to understand nonetheless, since we are all aware of the objective, the purpose and the goal sought after in a wrestling match.

Our first observation must surely be that wrestling is a very personal contest as it involves two individuals grappling with one another, the objective of which is to dominate and overthrow their opponent in this hand to hand conflict. It is a struggle in which each contestant seeks to employ their strength and their wits in order to accomplish this end, and therefore this conflict requires physical strength, quick reflexes and a series of moves carefully thought out and swiftly executed, moves which need to take into account the shape, size and ability of your opponent. Each contestant will seek to catch his opponent unawares, off guard and unprepared. Indeed, each contestant may invent a series of moves in his own mind designed to do just that.

That Satan has had great success here is seen in the number of Churches down through the centuries that began as a great threat to him while today the voice of the Lord from their pulpits is strangely silent.

The very fact that the Apostle sounds this note of warning in a universal manner and the fact that he uses the word 'we' in this verse (Ch. 6:12), indicates his firm belief that no Christian is exempt from this struggle. The question we all need to face is, 'are we still striving?' are we still wrestling? Are we still battling with all our might? Are we still struggling? Or, has Satan overcome us, has he won the bout? Has he outwitted us? Are we down? Have we decided to throw in the towel? Have we been immobilized, unable to beat the count? Are we ready to yield? For it is a fact that he has given many a saint of God a sore tumble. As the prophet Amos said, "Woe to those who are at ease in Zion." (Amos Ch. 6:1). We cannot afford to be taken by surprise.

Furthermore, in wrestling we not only have a trial of strength and courage; there is also the mental struggle that we must face. These struggles in life can leave us exhausted and weary, weakening our resolve to go on and Satan is not slow to seize upon this to his advantage. At such times we need to cast ourselves upon the Lord remembering what the apostle tells us at the very commencement of this passage, "Finally, my brethren, be strong in the Lord and in the power of His might." (verse 10). Indeed, at such a time, let us remember Israel's battle with the Amalekites; while those with Joshua were striving with their enemies in battle, Moses, helped by Aaron and Hur, were raising their hands to God in supplication to Him. We, too, require to do both.

As we noted earlier, part of the technique used in wrestling is to fool your opponent into thinking you are going to move in one direction whilst your intention is to move in the very opposite direction. All too often we are fooled into thinking that our enemy is coming at us from one direction while, in fact, he is preparing to attack us from another. In the realm of theology for example, the devil raises up teachers who teach some heresy or other provoking a response in which those, seeking to defend the truth, make the mistake of going too far in the opposite direction. An example of this is seen in the issue of legalism. There were some within the early Church who placed a wrong emphasis upon the law of God as it is found in the Old Testament. Unfortunately, there were some, seeking to avoid the danger of legalism, who, while seeking to emphasize the grace of God as against the emphasis on works, ended up promoting a form of antinomianism. Other areas of theology where this problem can be encountered regards the doctrine of the trinity, one God in three Persons; the relationship of the humanity and deity in the Person of Jesus Christ; the Person of the Holy Spirit and the relationship of God's sovereignty and human responsibility not to mention the issue of faith and works, etc.

Sad to say however, our striving is not always with the devil. Indeed, the problem with some of us is that we are too strong for our own good. Like Jacob, we trust to our own wits and devices to get what we want leading, on occasions, to the Lord having to wrestle with us as He did with Jacob in order to dry up our natural strength so that we might learn to lean upon the Lord's strength rather than upon our own since our greatest need in this life is to learn to lean upon Him and to learn to trust in Him. The Apostle Peter found this a painful lesson to learn.

Let us be careful then that we do not, through our own stubborn nature and unwillingness to accept God's will for our lives, find ourselves contending with God Himself. May our struggle always be with Satan and may we confine ourselves to that struggle we are bound to win (with God's help), rather than to the one we are bound to lose.

Chapter Five: The Prince and Power of Darkness

How many times have we heard it said, perhaps by a parent speaking of a strong willed child or by someone of a very close friend who was determined to follow a course which was clearly contrary to all good sense and one that would, inevitably, lead to a very sad and sorrowful conclusion, 'There is just no reasoning with them.'

What we intend by such a remark is that our child or friend is following a path which we truly believe will lead to a very painful end and where, for the moment at least, they are beyond the reach of argument or reasoning. They are unable to think about, or even discuss, the situation or issue in a reasonable manner. For the moment they are under the control of some very strong passion which appears to have all but taken them over making them unreasonable and unreachable. They are following a course of action which in their saner moments they would shudder to even contemplate. Nothing we can say, nothing we can do, is able to turn them from their fate. Indeed, is it not the case that at one time or another we have all been in that position, and that we have all had that said of us? Some sinful passion or desire has taken hold upon our heart and, for the moment, all right thinking has been abandoned or forsaken. We know that what we are doing is wrong and yet we choose to close our ears to every argument, every appeal made by others or even by our own conscience. The passion is there, it is powerful, it is persuasive and before long we find ourselves falling for the lies of the devil as Adam and Eve did so many years ago. They fell because they trusted in one they really did not know over against the One who had given them life. The story of the prodigal son provides us with yet another example of one who had to learn the hard way.

So, why is this? Why does it happen? Why are we so foolish and so stubborn? What explanation can we offer? These questions I believe can only be truly understood and addressed by the word of God, the Bible.

For example, in this very epistle we find a very helpful comment on the character and behavior of men; "And you He made alive, who were dead in trespasses and sins, in which you once walked according to the course of this world, according to the prince of the power of the air, the spirit who now works in the sons of disobedience, among whom also we all once conducted ourselves in the lusts of our flesh, fulfilling the desires of the flesh and of the mind, and were by nature children of wrath, just as the others." (Ch. 2:1-3)

However, what we need to take note of here is that not only do we have a reference to the serious, sinful condition of man which is big enough to destroy us but we also find a reference here to the influence in man of spiritual forces of evil we cannot see but which, nevertheless, exercise an influence and control upon us which only serves to compound an already existing problem.

It is a combination of these two facts that we find the answer or explanation for our condition. The natural, sinful passions found in man Satan appeals to in order to use to his advantage and it is under his influence that man tends to act in a most unreasonable and illogical manner, doing things, which, in his saner moments he would never dream of doing. An example of this is seen in the story of David and Bathsheba. At a time when kings go forth to war David is seen taking his ease lying on his couch or strolling on his roof top. His feet were not the only parts of his body that were wandering and thus his eyes caught sight of this very beautiful woman. The price he paid for his folly was great indeed. As the Lord said through Isaiah the prophet, "Hear, O heavens, and give ear, O earth! For the Lord has spoken: I have nourished and brought up children, and they have rebelled against Me; the ox knows it's owner and the donkey it's master's crib; but Israel does not know, My people do not consider." (Ch. 1:1-2) Truly, there is no reasoning with them. Nor does the Apostle leave us without an explanation for this as we see from this passage.

Having noted that we do not wrestle against flesh and blood, Paul goes on to say, "but against principalities, against powers, against the rulers of the darkness of this age, against spiritual hosts of wickedness in the heavenly places." Here, I believe, we have a word which holds the key to our understanding of so much that is taking place in the world around us and to the world within us.

The darkness he refers to here is not the darkness we are familiar with in the physical realm. He is merely borrowing language from the natural realm in order to convey to his readers a better understanding of the spiritual lessons and truths he is seeking to convey to them. Indeed, there are a number of helpful truths we can learn about the spiritual realm from a consideration of the natural realm.

[1.] Physical darkness is a realm in which man is not at home and for which he is ill equipped to dwell in. As the Lord said to His disciples before He raised Lazarus from the dead and in answer to a question put to Him by them, "Are there not twelve hours in the day? If anyone walks in the day, he does not stumble, because he sees the light of this world. But if one walks in the night, he stumbles, because the light is not in him." (John Ch. 11:9-10)

Now although the Lord was seeking to convey a spiritual truth to His disciples here, the fact is, man is not suited to live in darkness. There are some of God's creatures that are more suited to live in darkness than we are. Indeed, they function far better in the darkness than they do in the light.

[2.] Walking in the dark can be very dangerous in the natural realm. It becomes even more serious in the spiritual realm. Mans sight is very much more restricted and the deeper the darkness, the less he can see. We are aware that, in the natural world this can be very dangerous. A man may stumble and fall. Young David Balfour would have lost his life had it not been for the lightning flash. (Robert Louis Stevenson's 'Kidnapped') And many a sailor has given thanks to God for the light from the lighthouse warning them of the dangers ahead. Man would be very foolish to rush on in the darkness without taking due care. However, in the spiritual realm the dangers are greater still and yet, although men tend to show some caution in the natural realm, in the spiritual realm they are often very foolish. For they rush on blindly giving little thought on occasions to the dangers ahead and the awful consequences this path might lead to.

In his epistle to the Romans which is concerned with the issue of salvation, the Apostle Paul begins where every good preacher ought to begin; he looks at the need for salvation, and what he has to say is very helpful to us here since in the opening chapter he describes the path that man has chosen for himself and where it leads. "For the wrath of God is revealed from heaven against all ungodliness and unrighteousness of men, who suppress the truth in unrighteousness, because what may be known of God is manifest in them, for God has shown it to them. For, since the creation of the world His invisible attributes are clearly seen, being understood by the things that are made, even His eternal power and Godhead, so that they are without excuse, because, although they knew God, they did not glorify Him as God, nor were thankful, but became futile in their thoughts, and their foolish hearts were darkened. Professing to be wise, they became fools, etc." (Romans Ch.1:18-22).

Another passage is found in the Apostles second letter to the Corinthians where he refers to the fact that "we have renounced the hidden things of shame, not walking in craftiness nor handling the word of God deceitfully" after which he goes on to say that, "even if our gospel is veiled, it is veiled to those who are perishing, whose minds the god of this age has blinded, who do not believe, lest the light of the glory of Christ, who is the image of God, should shine on them. For we do not preach ourselves, but Christ Jesus the Lord, and ourselves your bondservants for Jesus sake. For it is the God who commanded light to shine out of darkness, who has shone in our hearts to give the light of the knowledge of the glory of God in the face of Jesus Christ." (2 Corinthians Ch.4:2-6) Nor is this darkness a mere consequence of sin so much as it is a deliberate choice on the part of man. Indeed, there is an astonishing statement found in the gospel of John that tells us, "Men loved darkness rather than light, because their deeds were evil." (Ch.3:19). And this is the only explanation for the state of the world we are living in today! Nor can man see where his sinful, godless life is taking him. Indeed, there is a dreadful example of what can happen found in the story of one of the disciples, Judas Iscariot, who was so near to the Lord during his ministry, and yet, on the night before the Lord was crucified, he chose to betray Him, but not before he observed the Passover with the Lord and His other disciples. And so it is that we have that very sad and ominous statement found in the thirteenth chapter, "Having received the piece of bread, he then went out immediately. And it was night!" (Ch.13:30).

From the above we see that men actually choose to live in ignorance of God. They choose darkness rather than light. Indeed they not only live in it, they love it; they prefer it. They choose to live in darkness because they know that what they are doing is wrong and yet, "knowing the righteous judgment of God, that those who practice such things are deserving of death, not only do the same but also approve of those who practice them." (Romans Ch.1:32).

When a man walks in darkness he is unable to see very clearly, if at all, what lies ahead. He may be conscious of shapes, forms and shadows but as to what they represent he is at a loss to know. He can only guess, which is exactly what most people do since we are unable to know with any certainty where our path may lead us.

In other words, darkness in the physical world involves a certain amount of ignorance which is why, when we are awakened by the gospel, we join with the psalmist in praying, "Oh, send out Your light and Your truth! Let them lead me; Let them bring me to Your holy hill and to Your tabernacle. Then I will go to the altar of God, to God my exceeding joy; and on the harp I will praise You, O God, my God." (Ps. 43:3-4). Nor is that the only place where light and truth are found together. In Psalm 119:105 we read, "Your word is a lamp to my feet and a light to my path." Furthermore, the bringing together of these two spiritual concepts, namely Gods' word and the light we receive at our conversion and the light we continue to receive throughout our Christian lives should not surprise us since the Lord Jesus Christ, who is the word of God become flesh, says of Himself, "I am the light of the world. He who follows Me shall not walk in darkness, but have the light of life." (Ch.8:12). And so, as we read in the opening chapter of John's gospel, "In the beginning was the Word, and the word was with God, and the Word was God. He was in the beginning with God…..In Him was life, and the life was the light of men. And the light shines in the darkness, and the darkness did not overcome it…..That was the true Light which gives light to every man coming into the world." (Ch. 1:1-5, 9).

However, it is not so much the darkness found in man that the Apostle is speaking of here as much as he is 'the spiritual hosts of wickedness' which are found 'in the heavenly places' described here as 'the rulers of the darkness of this age.' It is against these that we are struggling and it is with these that we are wrestling. We are opposed by these powers of darkness, because, first of all, they dwell in darkness. They themselves are ignorant, foolish, limited in their understanding, limited in their knowledge and limited in their vision. Only God is omniscient. Why else would Satan have entered the heart of Judas at that very moment which God had intended and ordained, in order to fulfill His great purpose and plan regarding the redemption of sinful men and women, not to mention the utter destruction of the devil himself; to deliver up the Lord into the hands of sinful men to be crucified at that very moment in history God had determined from before the foundation of the world. (Matt.Ch.25:34). By this action he only hastened his own demise!

Furthermore, they are called the powers of darkness not only because they dwell in darkness but also because, secondly, they deal in darkness. This is their goal, this is their task, to spread, to promote and to propagate as much spiritual darkness as they can. They are not only rulers in darkness they are the rulers of darkness. It is these wicked spirits who are responsible for all the lust, gross acts of indecency, adultery, human sacrifices, cannibalism, murder and all manner of wickedness, wars, and, as we see from this very letter, false teaching. As the Apostle said earlier, "This I say, therefore, and testify in the Lord, that you should no longer walk as the rest of the gentiles walk, in the futility of their mind, having their understanding darkened, being alienated from the life of God, because of the ignorance that is in them, because of the blindness of their heart; who, being past feeling, have given themselves over to lewdness, to work all uncleanness with greediness." (Ch.4:17-19). "For you were once darkness, but now you are light in the Lord. Walk as children of light (for the fruit of the Spirit is in all goodness, righteousness, and truth) finding out what is acceptable to the Lord. And have no fellowship with the unfruitful works of darkness, but rather expose them. For it is shameful even to speak of those things which are done by them in secret. But all things that are exposed are made manifest by the light for whatever makes manifest is light." (Ch.5:8-13).

We may not live any longer in the darkness as once we did but that does not mean that we cannot be guilty of some moral or spiritual failure at some point in our lives. The question we need to be asking then is this, where do we feel most comfortable? Where do we feel most at home? In the darkness or in the light?

Part Two: The Nature of The Christians' Armour

Chapter One: The Centrality of Truth

In coming to a consideration of the various items listed by the apostle that we are meant to put on as soldiers of Christ, perhaps, first of all, we should make an important observation with regard to the Christian Churches of today and that is that there appears to be very little mention of these items listed by the apostle, or of the spiritual warfare we have referred to earlier on, and so perhaps we ought ask the question, why?

In seeking to provide an answer we need to begin by noting that the passage currently under consideration is in two parts. There is first of all a general call to arms, an exhortation, to take up the whole armour of God in order to stand against the wiles of the devil. He then makes reference to the fact that we will be wrestling not against flesh and blood but against principalities and against the very powers of darkness. For in this we have both the reason and the purpose for this exhortation. Having issued this appeal, this exhortation, he then goes on to describe the various parts of the spiritual armour and makes clear to all who read this letter that they need to take unto themselves every item if they are to stand against the attacks of this very dangerous enemy. However, the failure of so many Christians and Churches in our day to heed this latter instruction, that is, to put on this spiritual armour provided by the Lord, would appear to indicate an utter failure to take the earlier words of the Apostle seriously concerning the demonic opposition we will inevitably encounter once we are saved! To speak of such things today is out of fashion. Surely the idea that demonic beings either do not exist or, at least, are very rarely involved in the life of the Church, or of the individual Christian, is the commonly held view of the majority of Christians today which would explain why there is so little concern regarding the Christian armour. After all, it would stand to reason that if what the apostle speaks of in the first part of this exhortation is not true, the latter part of this appeal would be rendered irrelevant.

The question therefore is this, 'do we believe, do we take seriously what the apostle is saying in these verses? Are we convinced that there are wicked spiritual beings seeking to oppose us, seeking to influence our thinking and our behavior, as to the decisions we make, the directions we take and the laws of God that they want us to break? Is this something we take seriously, or is it not?'

Do we truly believe that we are in a battle, that our lives are being lived in the midst of a terrible conflict being waged between God and Satan? Do we see history as the outworking of this struggle or as the happenings of chance?

Do we feel within ourselves something of the pressure and the tensions associated with this conflict? Are we aware of the seriousness of this situation? Do we ever feel ourselves drawn to do what is wrong when we know what is right and do we sometimes find ourselves doing what is right in spite of our inward passions tempting us to do what is wrong?

Is our understanding of man one which merely sees him as a physical being with chemical properties? Or do we believe that man is a physical being possessed of a spiritual nature living in a physical, material world where unseen spiritual beings seek to exert an untold influence upon that life, since nothing Paul says in these later verses will make any real impression upon us unless, or until, we accept what he has written in those earlier verses? For without that conviction there will be no sense of urgency to comply with these commands or instructions found in this passage.

Furthermore, is it not true to say that at a very early age, most of us, if not all of us, do become aware of a conflict within, a struggle between doing what we 'ought' to do and what we 'want to do'. Our conscience and our will are often seeking to guide us in very different directions. They are found to be contrary to one another. On the one hand we have to exercise self-control or, if we decide to go against our conscience, we have to find something to stifle its accusing voice or to put it to sleep while we act contrary to its will.

In other words, we have to justify our behavior, we have to rationalize our actions as Adam tried to do when he was confronted by the Lord in Eden. "The woman You gave to be with me," he said, "she gave me of the tree, and I ate." We know that we are in the wrong and that we are guilty. Nevertheless, we cannot bring ourselves to admit that we are, and so we try to find some reason or excuse, some justification, for what we have done. We try to rationalize our actions and therefore justify our behavior by shifting the blame to someone or even to something else, in order to avoid the truth. "And this is the condemnation, that the light has come into the world, and men loved darkness rather than light because their deeds were evil. For everyone practicing evil hates the light and does not come to the light, lest his deeds should be exposed. But he who does the truth comes to the light, that his deeds should be clearly seen, that they have been done in God." (John Ch.3:19-21).

All of which leads me to say that if the failure of the Christian Church to act in accordance with these instructions is anything to go by, and if the obvious failure of many professing Christians to arm themselves for the battle is indicative of our position, it must then be concluded that, today, very few Christians take the first part of this exhortation seriously. Indeed, very few Christians see themselves as being involved in a spiritual conflict at all; a state of affairs that could lead to the sweeping away of the Christian Church altogether. After all, no one can stand against an enemy he does not believe in! Only by Gods' grace can we survive.

It must also be said that even amongst those of us who do believe in the spiritual forces of evil, and of the opposition arrayed against us, there is still a need to be reminded of our duty to take our stand and to be prepared for this conflict.

All too often, those of us who do believe, behave as though we did not. We can forget for a while and become so engrossed in the ordinary affairs of life we need to be reminded of the opposition we are called upon to engage on a daily basis. Indeed, this appeal to clothe ourselves with the armour that the Lord has provided in order that we may stand would seem to imply that if we fail to obey this instruction, we will be unable to stand and will, therefore, be defeated.

It should be no surprise therefore to find that the very first piece of the Christians armour is the girdle of truth to be worn around the waist. This indicates just how important and fundamental this whole issue of truth and error, darkness and light, really is. The

Christian life begins when we are awakened by the truth and to the truth. As the Lord said, "You will know the truth and the truth will set you free." (John Ch.8:32).

Before we can take our place in the ranks as soldiers of Christ therefore, we must first of all put on the whole armour of God, for only then will we ever be able to stand against the wiles of the devil; and the very first piece of that armour is this girdle of truth which may not seem to be a part of the soldiers' armour at all. However, as we see throughout the scriptures, truth is both foundational and fundamental. Truth and light stand opposed to error and darkness. Indeed, in this contrast we have a most penetrating insight into the world around us. We are living in the midst of a major battlefield where truth and error, darkness and light are joined in a conflict, a spiritual battle which is being waged between the Spirit of God on the one hand and the demonic spirits that serve the devil on the other; which is why we need to realise that whenever we encounter false doctrine, whether in the falsehood of the cults or even within the Christian Church itself, we need to recognise that these doctrines are the doctrines of demons and must not be treated lightly. We are living in the midst of a spiritual war being waged between demonic forces and the Son of God, the end of which has already been determined.

The sinner is saved by receiving the truth. As the Saviour said, "And you shall know the truth, and the truth shall make you free." (John Ch.8:32). Indeed, in that same chapter He said, "Therefore if the Son makes you free, you shall be free indeed." (verse 36). Whereas, He spoke directly to those who rejected Him saying, "You are of your father the devil, and the desires of your father you want to do. He was a murderer from the beginning, and does not stand in the truth, because there is no truth in him. When he speaks a lie, he speaks from his own resources, for he is a liar and the father of it." (verse 44). And so in the work of salvation we must begin with the gospel and the preaching of the truth. And once we have been saved it is vital that we continue to gird ourselves with the truth since it alone can preserve us from error.

We need to remember that it was right here that it all began to go wrong for us. We believed a lie rather than the truth. Here, therefore, is where we must begin in the process of salvation. Having received the truth of the gospel we must ensure that we continue in the truth and grow, both in the knowledge of the gospel and in the knowledge of the Lord. This is why, when the Apostle Paul is ready to move on from the general exhortation in order to deal with the specific items one by one, he begins with the girdle of truth. He desires to exhort those early Christians to put on each piece of the armour he lists here, in the order he lists here, that they may be able to stand against the wiles of the devil. The very order is important, which is why, when he comes to deal with the specific items one by one, he begins with the girdle of truth.

Another passage of scripture which is extremely helpful to us here is found in the first letter of the apostle Peter and in the opening chapter where he addresses the exiles of the dispersion whose faith was being severely 'grieved by various trials.' His advice to them was connected to this very issue referred to by the apostle Paul in the passage we are looking at in Ephesians; Peters' advice was, "Therefore gird up the loins of your mind, etc." (verse 13).

In the letter to the Ephesians we understand the girdle to refer to the truth ("having girded your waist with truth,)" whereas in the apostle Peters' letter our waist or loins refers to our mind, ("gird up the loins of your mind").

The above is extremely helpful to us, first of all in seeking to expound, and secondly to explain the Apostle Paul's statement in the passage before us. As the Roman soldier of that day began his preparations by gathering up the loose garments around his waist for the sake of security and stability so the Christian must be careful to ensure that his thinking and mental preparation is not uncertain as regards the truth of scripture. He must know what he believes and no Christian should ever take this issue lightly since his spiritual life will depend on it.

As the Roman soldier began to prepare for the coming conflict by securing his clothing, so too, the Christian must be in no doubt as to what he, or she, believes. If we hold fast to the truth we will soon discover that the truth will hold us fast!

It is also not without significance that the area covered here is the most sensitive part of the body. We may have made the common mistake of thinking that the most sensitive and the most vulnerable part of our body is our heart. Clearly, the apostles were more concerned to guard our thinking, to guard our minds first and foremost, for this in turn will affect our hearts.

Furthermore, we need to understand that men were not ignorant in regard to truth and error. Men chose of their own volition to reject the truth and to believe the lies of Satan. As the Apostle Paul tells us in the opening chapter of his letter to the Romans, "For the wrath of God is revealed from heaven against all ungodliness and unrighteousness of men, who suppress the truth in unrighteousness, for what may be known of God is manifest in them, for God has shown it to them. For since the creation of the world, His invisible attributes are clearly seen, being understood by the things that are made, even His eternal power and Godhead, so they are without excuse, because, although they knew God, they did not glorify Him as God, nor were thankful, but became futile in their thoughts, and their foolish hearts were darkened. Professing to be wise they became fools and changed the glory of the incorruptible God into an image made like corruptible man……Therefore God also gave them up to uncleanness, etc. " (Romans. Ch.1:18-24). He goes on, "For this reason God gave them up to vile passions…….and even as they did not like to retain God in their knowledge, God gave them over to a debased mind, to do those things that are not fitting; being filled with all unrighteousness, sexual immorality, wickedness, covetousness, maliciousness; full of envy, murder, strife, deceit, evil-mindedness; they are whisperers, backbiters, haters of God, violent, proud, boasters, inventors of evil things, disobedient to parents, undiscerning, unmerciful: who knowing the righteous judgment of God, that those who practice such things are deserving of death, not only do the same but also approve of those who practice them." (verses 26-32).

From this we see that man is not ignorant of the truth, rather, he does not want to hear it and is totally opposed to it. Due to their love of sin and self they wish to put the truth as far away from themselves as they can. And so it is, before the work of restoration and reformation begins in the life of a sinner, there must be a complete turnaround in regard to this matter of the truth. It must be acknowledged, recognised, accepted, adhered to and adopted as the standard by which all things must be judged.

Indeed, as we see from this passage, the truth must not only be embraced by us but we ourselves must be embraced by the truth. It must be allowed to put its strong arms around us in order to hold us fast in the coming conflict for a conflict there will certainly be if we are truly saved!

Indeed, the importance of right doctrine cannot be underestimated. Of the various letters found in the New Testament, nearly all have something to say about the dangers of false doctrine. Indeed, we see that some of the strongest words of condemnation are found in connection with those who peddle their false teachings in the Churches founded by the apostles. It was, perhaps, the single greatest threat to the Christian Church then. Indeed, it is probably true to say that it is still the single greatest threat to the Christian Church of today.

Modern scholarship is just one example of this threat. Some scholars even go so far as to say that the scriptures are not infallible. But if that is true, what then do they make of the statement found in the opening chapter of Johns' gospel (Ch.1:14), "And the Word became flesh and dwelt among us, and we beheld His glory, the glory as of the only begotten of the Father, full of grace and truth." Was Christ full of error? Indeed, they are sure that, today, due to modern scholarship, they are ar better informed as to the teaching of Gods' word than those who went before us. For example, does the scripture say that men love darkness rather than light? Not at all! What it ought to say is that man loves light rather than darkness and is searching earnestly for it. Does it teach us that there is none righteous, no not one? Not true, they tell us. There are many good people in the world even if they do not embrace the teaching of the bible as we do. Does the scripture say that Jesus, alone, is the Way, the Truth and the Life and that no one comes to the Father except through Him? What He meant to say is that all who are sincere, all who are religious, shall come to the Father for there are many roads and routes to heaven. Did the Lord say 'come ye out from among them and be separate'? Well, this is clearly wrong. Instead we are to come together and bury our differences since they are the cause of so much trouble and division in our world. We need to repent and embrace those who once differed from us and with whom we were not able to have true fellowship. Are we not to allow them into our homes or bid them God speed? Why, that is contrary to all that is Christian. We need to talk to them; we need to listen to them and we need to try to understand them in order to find some middle ground. After all no one has a monopoly of the truth. To take a firm line is to be bigoted and that is just not Christian.

Now the truth referred to here is not to the evangelistic message we are to take to others so much as that gospel by which we ourselves have been saved, that truth we have been embraced by and which we are now urged to hold fast. There is no room here for loose thinking in regard to that work of grace which has been wrought in our hearts or to that truth by which that work of grace was accomplished, for Satan will always create the greatest disturbance wherever or whenever the truth is either ignored or forgotten or both. How often do we see the apostle Paul addressing his epistles to the Christians of that time whether in dealing with the practical problems or to the theological issues of their day with questions such as, "Do you not know?" Letters like Romans, Corinthians, Galatians and Hebrews all testify to the same thing whether in regard to theological, or with regard to practical, issues. The underlying problem can be traced back to this one failure, a lack of knowledge.

What the apostle is saying here may be described as some of the most vital words of instruction to be found in scripture next to the message of the gospel. Satan is real. His desire and design is to destroy us all and it is only by following these words of instruction that we can be preserved.

This item of clothing was the first item of clothing worn by the Roman soldier as he began to prepare for battle. It, in itself, was not a part of the armour either for offence or defense. Nevertheless, it was, in itself, a vital part of the soldiers' clothing as it allowed him to move quickly and with greater confidence providing both security and stability.

The devil is only too well aware of the importance of truth and of its power to awaken the sinner to their need of a Saviour. From the very beginning he has sought to deceive us with his wickedness; sowing seeds of doubt first of all upon what God had said and then by openly contradicting what He had said; "Has God said?" followed by, "You shall not die!" He knows that the fear of the Lord is the beginning of wisdom and thus must do all that he can to prevent man from ever trusting the word of God. He will deny it, denounce it, distort it, defy it and even attempt to destroy it, if possible, and if none of these succeed he will seek to distract us and discourage us from reading it or divert our attention away from it when it is being read as often as he can, for there can be no doubt that Satan creates the greatest disturbance whenever and wherever the truth is ignored or forgotten!

Of course, there can be no doubt that one of the greatest threats to the Christian church in our day is found in regard to this very issue. A war is being waged against what some would deem as old fashioned, out dated and ancient traditions that, according to them, have no place today in our brave new world where the key word is not 'truth' but 'love.'

During the 1960's there was a slogan that the young people of that era made popular which said, "Make Love, Not War." Understandable perhaps given the fact we had just come through two world wars, another war in Korea and one of the worst of them for the U.S.A., the war in Vietnam!

Everyone wanted peace; people had had enough of conflict and suffering. They wanted to enjoy life again and the benefits of a more affluent society.

During those dreadful years of conflict, the Christian church had played a very important role in the hearts and homes of those whose loved ones had been involved in those awful conflicts; a legacy of which was the connection between Church going and the personal suffering they had gone through. Their memories were still fresh and hard to bear. Add to this the whole question of suffering and evil and we have another reason for the drop in Church membership and Church going.

In seeking to remedy this change in peoples' habits on Sundays many chose to preach a rather different message, one of joy and hope instead of a call to repentance which would have been a more biblical approach after all that the world had recently endured. That such preaching might not be heard willingly may indeed be true; we will never know as that was not the message they chose to preach in the end. "Make love, not war" had won the day, the ears and the hearts of that generation. Perhaps they may have been better to turn to the words of another song writer from a bygone era, King Solomon no less whose advice to us all is diametrically opposed to, 'Make Love Not War.' "A good name is better than precious ointment, and the day of death than the day of one's birth; Better to go to the house of mourning than to go to the house of feasting for that is the end of all men; and the living will take it to heart."

One of the great problems with the human race is their uncanny habit to swing like a pendulum and soon we were staring at a moral landslide in the world around us which soon penetrated the ranks of the Christian Church and threatens, even now, to destroy it. For, in seeking to be acceptable to the world of our day we are not only expected to accept forms of immorality condemned by the word of God such as homosexuality (and other forms of sexual perversity) into our churches but we are expected to welcome them into our pulpits as well! In addition to this we also have women intruding upon the office of preacher and teacher, a role they are forbidden to take in the scriptures. All of this is not compromising so much as capitulating. As we read in Isaiah Ch. 5:20 "Woe to those who call evil good, and good evil", for that is exactly what they are doing.

To play fast and loose with the word of God is utter madness. As someone once said, 'The purpose of preaching is to comfort the afflicted and to afflict the comfortable.' While many preachers are doing their best to convince the sinner that God loves them, the word of God is seeking to convict them as sinners in order to bring them to repentance so that once they have repented, they may be comforted! After all you cannot have conversion without conviction. In the garden of Eden the Lord confronted Adam and Eve in regard to their nakedness; in 2 Samuel Ch.12:7 the Lord, through Nathan the prophet, confronted David in the matter of his sin with Bathsheba and her husband Uriah.

To these examples we may add that of the Samaritan woman Christ meets at the well (John Ch.4) or even the rich young ruler who went away sorrowful as many have done from our churches when the cost of true discipleship has become clear to them, sad to say.

As the Roman soldier takes that first step in preparing for the battle ahead by the girding up of his loins, so too, every soldier of Christ must ensure that he girds up his mind with the truth of Gods' word, convinced of its' truthfulness and its' importance in regard to his duty to stand against the wiles of the devil.

As soldiers of Christ do we keep silent when we are in the company of those who do not believe when biblical issues are being discussed or do we stand our ground as the Lord leads us, regardless of the outcome and regardless of the cost to ourselves. Indeed, do we guard ourselves against the temptation to focus on all the blessings of the Christian life and avoid anything that might lead to controversy which might put us out of favour with that particular set of friends. As the hymn puts it, 'Who is on the Lord's side, who will face the foe?' One thing is certain, we will need to gird ourselves with the truth of Gods' word if we are ever to stand our ground!

Chapter Two: The Breastplate of Righteousness

In coming to the second item the apostle refers to here, the breastplate of righteousness, some may wish to suggest that this is, in effect, the first piece of armour as the 'girdle' or girding of the loins is not strictly an item of armour, even although we recognise it to be a necessary part of the preparation of the soldier for the conflict. However, since the conflict we are preparing for here is a spiritual conflict, I would suggest that the girdle of truth is a very real and a very necessary part of the Christian soldiers' armour to protect us against the wiles of the devil. This ought to be clear to anyone who reads the New Testament. I will therefore refer to the breastplate of righteousness as the second item every Christian soldier needs to put on in order to be able to stand against the attacks of the enemy.

It should also be noted that in our reading of the scriptures we very soon discover that there are only two ways for a man to become righteous. The first is by keeping the commandments of God perfectly, which none of us can, whereas, the only other way is by Another, keeping the law perfectly on our behalf, and then, having paid the penalty for our sins in full, accrediting us with His sinless, righteous and perfect life as we come to Him by faith and receive Him as our Saviour. Nor is that faith, by which we believe, a faith that finds its' source in us or from us, "For by faith you have been saved, and that not of yourselves; it is the gift of God, not of works, lest anyone should boast." (Eph. Ch.2:8-9).

An illustration or example of the above can be seen in the story of the Fall found in Genesis where, having sinned, Adam and his wife Eve sought, first of all, to cover their own nakedness from one another after which they sought to hide from the presence of the

Lord as many attempt to do still. This covering was clearly unacceptable to God and so He removed the aprons of fig leaves, thus exposing their shame and nakedness since no one is able to hide the truth of their sinful condition from the eyes of Him with whom we have to do. The covering we require is not only a gift of Gods' grace but one which must be taken from another only after they have been put to death.

Furthermore, it must also be noted that there are two areas of concern in regard to this issue of righteousness, both of which we need to consider as Christians. In the first place we need to acknowledge that there is a righteousness that must be imputed; that is, as the Lord Jesus gives to us His righteousness and takes upon Himself our sin thus making saints out of sinners. However, imputed righteousness is not the only concern of the true believer, or of the gospel. There is also the need to have that righteousness imparted. We are accepted in the Beloved according to Gods' grace. Nevertheless, we are also to be holy because He is holy. We are not to continue in sin that grace may abound but to put off the old man with his deeds and pursue holiness without which no man shall see God.

It is also very important to understand that the Christian soldier requires to have both that righteousness which is imputed to us and that righteousness which is imparted to us when facing the devil. The apostle John describes him in Revelation as the accuser of the brethren "Then I heard a loud voice saying in heaven, 'Now salvation, and strength, and the kingdom of our God, and the power of His Christ have come, for the accuser of our brethren, who accused them before our God day and night, has been cast down.'" (Ch.12:10).

An example of this very thing is found in the account of the prophet Zechariah concerning Joshua the high priest; "Then he showed me Joshua the high priest standing before the Angel of the Lord, and Satan standing by his right hand to oppose him. And the Lord said to Satan, 'The Lord rebuke you, Satan! The Lord who has chosen Jerusalem rebuke you! Is this not a brand plucked from the fire?'" (Zechariah Ch.3:1-5).

The apostle Paul understood this truth as we see in his letter to the Christians in Rome. "What then shall we say to these things? If God is for us, who can be against us? He who did not spare His own Son, but delivered Him up for us all, how shall He not with Him also freely give us all things? Who shall bring a charge against God's elect?" (Our enemy Satan will of course, but not successfully as the apostle goes on to explain) "It is God who justifies. Who is he who condemns? It is Christ who died, and furthermore is also risen, who is even at the right hand of God, who also makes intercession for us." Imputed righteousness is the reason our enemy will not and cannot succeed. Nor can he succeed in creating a breech in our ranks with this approach so long as this important truth of scripture is known and trusted by the believer. The Lord has made provision for us and in this, our deliverance is found and our peace is assured.

However, if the devil cannot unsettle us in regard to the issue of imputed righteousness, he may find that in the matter of imparted righteousness he may have greater success and a greater opportunity since in this issue Christians can be very vulnerable indeed. As we read through the New Testament we see that the apostles have good reason for concern over the behavior of so many believers. If we do not apply the truths of scripture to the way that we live we will very soon discover our inability to stand against the wiles of the devil.

Moving on from there and looking more directly at this item, the breastplate of righteousness, I have to confess that the more I study these verses at the end of this letter of Paul's, the more I am convinced we are dealing with one of the most important passages to be found in the New Testament. This is due, in part, to the subject it addresses, namely, the whole issue of the spiritual warfare we all face as Christians from the moment we come to the Lord in repentance and faith until that day when we enter the presence of God in glory. Indeed, in all probability, we may already have faced some serious opposition even prior to our receiving Christ as our Saviour.

However, it is also due to the fact that the process of putting on the spiritual armour is a setting forth of the process by which the sinner is saved for, as we look a little closer at the various pieces of the armour and the order in which they are referred to here, we notice an amazing resemblance to the process by which the Lord brings the sinner to repentance; beginning, as we see, with the truth. The work of salvation and the saving of the sinner always begins with the conviction that the Bible is nothing more and nothing less than God's word, His truth. This is the very means by which the Lord awakens the sinner to their need of salvation. It enters the mind to instruct us, it enters the heart to awaken us and it enters the soul to transform us creating life where there was death and bringing light to where there was only darkness.

We also need reminding that the breastplate of righteousness is not made, produced or fashioned by the sinner. The Lord alone was able to live the perfect life of righteousness in order to procure this item of armour for us. It is a gift of God's grace and yet, as we see from the words of command, the Christian soldier must recognise that it is we, ourselves, who are responsible to "put on the whole armour of God" and, "having put on the breastplate of righteousness" implies that it is the one wearing it who puts it on.

In the gospels we see that prior to His arrest, the Lord took time to further instruct His disciples as to what would happen once He was taken from them. "But now I go away to Him who sent Me, and none of you asks Me, 'Where are You going?' But because I have said these things to you, sorrow has filled your heart. Nevertheless I tell you the truth. It is to your advantage that I go away; for if I do not go away, the Helper will not come to you; but if I depart, I will send Him to you. And when He has come, <u>He will convict the world of sin, and of righteousness</u>, and of judgment: of sin, because they do not believe on Me; of righteousness because I go to My Father and you see Me no more; of judgment because the ruler of this world is judged. I still have many things to say to you, but you cannot bear them now. However, when He, the Spirit of truth has come, He will guide you into all truth."(John Ch.16:5-13). The fact is, as we see from the above, the truth alone is insufficient since truth is not an end in itself but a means to an end. It comes to awaken us, it comes to convict us; it comes as an instrument of God to convert us. As we see from the account of the temptation of the Lord, even Satan knows the scriptures.

Having achieved this end in the salvation of the sinner, the purpose of God is now to use the truth in order to sanctify His people, to make them holy, for this is one of the great goals of salvation as we see from the Lord's prayer to His Father recorded by the apostle John, "Sanctify them by Your truth. Your word is truth."(Ch.17:17). And in this very epistle of Paul to the Ephesians we find another helpful statement, "Husbands, love your wives, just as

Christ also loved the Church and gave Himself for her, that He might sanctify and cleanse her with the washing of water by the word."(Ch.5:25-26). As one preacher put it, 'truth is the root of which righteousness is the fruit.' The one should lead inevitably to the other.

Nor is the idea of this being a dual effort a novel one as we are exhorted in Paul's letter to the Philippians, "Therefore, my beloved, as you have always obeyed, not as in my presence only, but now much more in my absence, work out your own salvation with fear and trembling; for it is God who works in you both to will and to do for His good pleasure."

God's great purpose is to oppose and reverse the work of sin; to unite where sin divides, to set free those who were bound, to restore where sin destroyed and to pardon those who were under the condemnation of the law in order that they should live lives of godliness and holiness. For the one thing that Satan hates and fears more than the truth, is the truth supported by the lives of godly men and women. Truth, alone, accurate as it may be, should always be supported by a life lived in the light of that truth. People listen to what we say and then they look at us to see how we live. Is there really a God to whom I can turn? Is sin really that serious? And what about the Lord Jesus, is He really the best friend a sinner like me can trust? Are Christians really honest, faithful, trustworthy and caring? The world needs to see Christ in us as well as hearing about Christ from us. Do these Christians really take the message of the gospel seriously? The Jews of Jesus' day had the oracles of God but it made little difference to the way they lived. God's truth, when embraced by faith, should always result in a godly life; truth should always lead to righteousness. Truth is the root of which righteousness is the fruit.

As to the spiritual message, meaning and importance of the breastplate and of the purpose of the apostle in referring to this item here, we see that the breastplate was that part of the soldiers armour which guarded, among other things, the heart of the soldier since this is one of the major targets the enemy aims to pierce and, thus, in the spiritual conflict, Satan employs his very best storm troopers to mount an attack and even lay siege to it over a long period of time in order to strike a fatal blow. In attacking the heart Satan's objective is to turn our affections away from the Lord; to incite us to rebellion as he did with our first parents in Eden. In Proverbs we read, "My son, give attention to my words; incline your ear to my sayings. Do not let them depart from your eyes; keep them in the midst of your heart; for they are life to those who find them, and health to all their flesh. Keep your heart with all diligence, for out of it are the issues of life." (Prov. Ch.4:20-23). As the Lord said to the disciples as recorded in Matthew's gospel, "For out of the heart proceed evil thoughts, murders, adulteries, fornications, thefts, false witness, blasphemies. These are the things that defile a man, etc." (Matt. Ch.15:19-20). How careful we need to be! Indeed, in that very same chapter in Matthew the Lord, quoting from the prophet Isaiah, said, "These people draw near to Me with their mouth, and honor Me with their lips, but their heart is far from Me." (Isaiah Ch.29:13 and Matthew Ch.15:8). From the passage above in Proverbs we see that the responsibility for guarding our hearts is ours. Indeed, this can be said of every item of the Christian armour.

Furthermore, if we take time to study the art of warfare we will soon deduce that when one army throws the weight of their attack in one direction it is for two reasons at least; the vulnerability and the strategic importance of their enemies position; which is why the Lord in the promises found in the books of Jeremiah and Ezekiel speaks of a New Covenant in which He promises to give to His people a new heart; "I will give you a new heart and put a new spirit within you; I will take the heart of stone out of your flesh and give you a heart of flesh. I will put My Spirit within you and cause you to walk in My statutes, and you will keep My judgments and do them." (Ezekiel Ch.36:26-27 see also Jeremiah Ch.31:31-32).

Since the devil cannot prevent the Lord from giving us a new heart he will do all that he can to prevent us from living in accordance with His will as expressed in His word. The church in Ephesus is an example of this as we see in the book of Revelation and the second chapter. Through time this congregation, though commended for their works, their labor, their patience as well as their ability to discern, and unwillingness to tolerate those who were evil, yet, had this against them, that they had lost their first love (Ch.2:4).

There are many reasons why we should strive after holiness. We should seek it first of all because without it we will not see the Lord. (Hebrews Ch.12:14). We should also strive after holiness because it is Gods' will that we should be holy. Thirdly, we should pursue holiness because the Lord Jesus was crucified and died in order to make us holy. It cost Him His life.

Furthermore, we should be holy because it is in our best interest to be holy; Gods' blessing, His favor, His kindness and His rewards are reserved for those who seek to be holy even as He is holy. As we are told in the apostle's letter to young Timothy, "Now godliness with contentment is great gain." (1 Tim. Ch. 6:6). And in addition to the above we may add that the Lord intends that we should bear witness to His saving grace by our being the salt of the earth, the light of the world and a city set on a hill that cannot be hidden. We are to be His witnesses! And this is what makes this whole issue of righteousness so very important. In other words we are to be holy, godly and righteous since it is Gods' purpose and plan that by this means we should bear witness to the truthfulness of our message. For this is surely what the Lord meant when He said in the sermon on the mount, "you are the salt of the earth", "the light of the world", "a city set on a hill that cannot be hidden (Matt. Ch. 5:13-14). We are to be His witnesses. In us He demonstrates what He can do for others and through us He speaks to the world.

Indeed, this is what makes the possession of righteousness so important. Next to the gospel message itself it is the best weapon we have against Satan and his wickedness which is why he attacks the Christian church with such vigor and such ferocity. The man or woman who lives according to the teaching of this book and seeks to be Christ like is the greatest threat to Satan next to the word of God itself.

Satan will stop at nothing in his desire and eagerness to overthrow our witness, to discredit our testimony and to counter the effect of God's work of grace in our lives. A truly Christian life is an effective witness as Satan knows only too well and it is for this reason he seeks to sow his tares amongst the wheat. He would undermine and compromise our witness; one good reason why we should pursue holiness and righteousness.

Chapter Three: The Gospel of Peace

In moving on to the third item of spiritual armour referred to here by the apostle Paul, namely, the spiritual footwear to be worn by the Christian soldier preparing for battle, it is important, if we are to appreciate and understand the apostle's instructions, to remind ourselves of two very important aspects of this message; namely, the overall or wider context of this exhortation which has to do with the unity Christ died to secure, a unity we need to guard with every fiber of our being against the wiles of the devil, followed by a consideration of the more immediate context of this appeal in regard to this call to arms, addressed to every Christian and every congregation of God's people through this epistle, to prepare for this inevitable, and unavoidable, spiritual conflict which lies before us. As we see, the language used here is not so much the language of the spiritual pilgrim as it is the language of the Christian soldier. For, as the apostle writes elsewhere, "But you, O man of God………. Fight the good fight of faith", etc. (I Tim. Ch.6:11-12). As the apostle Peter wrote, "Beloved, do not think it strange concerning the fiery trial which is to try you, as though some strange thing happened to you…" (1 Peter Ch.4:12); and as our Lord said, "In the world you will have tribulation, but be of good cheer, I have overcome the world." (John Ch.16:33).

In addition to the above, we also need to consider the order in which the apostle lists these items of armour as there are some important lessons to be learned from this also.

Beginning then with the overall message of the epistle, or the wider aspect of it, we see that what the apostle is concerned to address here is the whole issue of our unity as Christians, since, as we have already considered, it is part of a general exhortation which the apostle addresses to the Christians in Ephesus towards the end of this particular epistle, with specific reference to the central theme found in every chapter throughout this letter, namely, the whole question of our unity since it is such a vital part of our witness to the gospel. The Lord Jesus died, not only to save sinners and to reconcile us to Himself, but to reconcile us to one another. He died for His bride, for the Christian Church, in order that through them He might be made known to the world in which we live. We are to go into all the world with the message of the gospel and in order for us to do this more effectively, it is important that we do more than preach a message of reconciliation, we must also manifest that reconciliation to those we seek to reach with our message. We must live together in harmony, in unity, manifesting that oneness which the Lord prayed for in the prayer He addressed to His Father prior to His crucifixion, "Now I am no longer in the world, but these are in the world, and I come to you. Holy Father, keep through Your name those whom You have given Me, that they may be one as We are...... I do not pray for these alone, but also for those who will believe in Me through their word; that they all may be one, as You, Father, are in Me, and I in You; that they also may be one in Us, that the world may believe that You sent Me. And the glory that You gave Me I have given them, that they may be one just as We are one: I in them, and You in Me; that they may be made perfect in one, and that the world may know that You have sent Me, and have loved them as You have loved Me." (John Ch.17:11, 20-23). It is important to bear this in mind when we come to consider this next item of armour on the list that the apostle gives to us here in this final appeal. Before we do, however, it is also important to recall the more immediate concern of the apostle here.

As we move on then to this second aspect or the more immediate context, it is important for us to appreciate and understand the contribution that this item of armour makes to the overall message and, consequently, it is important to recall what that more immediate setting or the more immediate context of this appeal or exhortation is; the need to be prepared for the spiritual warfare awaiting us once we are saved. And this we will do in a moment. However, before we turn to a consideration of this issue it needs to be said and it needs to be recognised, that the conflict referred to here is not a possibility, it is a certainty, for the moment we are saved we become a target for the devil and for all who serve him. It is therefore a very important matter and one we all need to be prepared to take very seriously. Putting on the spiritual armour is not an optional extra but a very basic requirement. If we fail to take the apostles' instructions seriously; and if we do not heed the apostles' exhortation to put on this armour, it can only mean one of two things; either we were never truly saved in the first place or else we are already overcome, we are already defeated, unwilling to take up our cross, living in disobedience to the Lords' will and word, living lives that are ineffective, without the battles, perhaps, but also without the blessings, similar to the seed that did not have much soil and dried up and died in the heat of the day when the sun rose.

Therefore, bearing all of the above in mind, we are now better prepared to come to a consideration of the more immediate concern, which is, the putting on of the spiritual armour for the spiritual warfare that lies ahead. In doing so, we need to ponder what it is the apostle is saying about the various items referred to in this passage. The true believer, the Christian who is truly committed and desires to serve the Lord, will not hurry past such a passage as this but will desire to consider what the apostle is saying here in order to understand Gods' will for us since these instructions are not the product of the apostles' over active imagination or the result or effect of a life of trials, opposition and persecution, but a part of the inspired record, inspired by the Holy Spirit Himself. Each item of armour has a spiritual parallel and a spiritual application. As said above, even the order in which they are presented to us has significance as I hope to demonstrate. No Christian can afford to treat this passage lightly.

Turning then to the item itself we see that, as with the first two items we have already considered, this third item referred to here is also concerned with our ability to 'stand' as we see in verse fifteen; "having shod your feet with the preparation of the gospel of peace"; a verse which, inserted here, suggests that this item is very important in our attempt to withstand our adversary, so much so, I have come to the conclusion that, in the light of the present state of the Christian Church, there can hardly be a more important or more relevant verse in the scriptures than this one. Having our 'feet shod' with the 'gospel of peace' is a very necessary part of our 'preparation' for the conflict ahead. It is an essential part of our spiritual armour. So what exactly is the apostle referring to here?

In the days of the Roman Empire the footwear of the soldier was a vital part of his armour. Sometimes, in pursuit of the enemy, they would have to travel some distance in order to engage them in battle and so they would need sandals or shoes that would not wear out easily. The safety and security of their feet was also of great importance in close conflict with their foe, and, due to the differing terrain, their feet needed to be comfortable and properly protected in order to stand their ground. Studs or nails were used to give the Roman soldier a better foothold when engaging the enemy. The footwear was essential, therefore, since it gave the soldier both security and mobility. After all, an army unable to stand, is an army unable fight.

It needs to be borne in mind of course that the apostle is not concerned in this passage with the task of evangelism wherein we seek to enter the devils kingdom in order to win souls to Christ, but with the need to stand firm against his attempts to disrupt and destroy, if he can, that oneness and that unity the Lord died to produce, provide and protect. We are to guard it and we must seek to protect it against all the efforts of the devil, and they are many, as he seeks to create division in our ranks; in our churches, in our families, in our friendships and even in our own personal lives.

And so it is we need to be able to stand our ground. We need to be secure, not easily moved away from the truth of the gospel. As the apostle wrote to the church in Colosse, "For it pleased the Father that in Him all the fullness should dwell, and by Him to reconcile all things to Himself, by Him, whether things on earth or things in heaven, having made peace through the blood of His cross. And you, who once were alienated and enemies in your mind by wicked works, yet now He has reconciled in the body of His flesh through death, to present you holy, and blameless, and above reproach in His sight – <u>if indeed you continue in the faith, grounded and steadfast, and are not moved away from the hope of the gospel which you heard</u> (Ch. 1:19-23). This is a danger we need to avoid at all costs!

Nor was the church in Ephesus the only Christian church the apostle was concerned about regarding this danger. Earlier on he had written a letter to all the churches in Galatia with a very strong message. "I marvel that you are turning away so soon from Him who called you in the grace of Christ, to a different gospel, which is not another; but there are some who trouble you and want to pervert the gospel of Christ. But even if we or an angel from heaven, preach any other gospel to you than what we have preached to you, let him be accursed. As we have said before, so now I say again, if anyone preaches any other gospel to you than what we have received, let him be accursed."

"For do I now persuade men, or God? Or do I now seek to please men? For if I still pleased men, I would not be a bondservant of Christ."

Furthermore, this work of reconciliation was not confined to the relationship between God and sinful men as we see in an earlier statement found in this very epistle where we read; "For He Himself is our peace, who has made both one, and has broken down the middle wall of separation, having abolished in His flesh the enmity, that is, the law of commandments contained in ordinances, so as to create in Himself one new man from the two, thus making peace, and that He might reconcile them both to God in one body through the cross, thereby putting to death the enmity. <u>And He came and preached peace to you who were afar off and to those who were near</u>. For through Him we both have access by one Spirit to the Father." (Ch.2:14-18).

And so it was, among the many things our Lord accomplished by His death on the cross, as we see from the gospel records, was that He made peace through the blood of His cross; peace between God and His people and peace between His saints; a peace we need to guard with all our might. After all, as we have already noted that the Lord said in His prayer in John chapter seventeen, "I do not pray for these alone, but also for those who will believe in Me through their word; that they all may be one, as You, Father are in Me, and I in You; that they also may be one in Us, that the world may believe that You sent Me." (Verses 20-21). Living together in peace and harmony is not only the great concern of this epistle to the Ephesians, but is one of the major reasons why Satan attacks us. He knows how important the unity of the Christian church is to the credibility of our message.

From the early days of the apostles to the present day Satan has done his utmost to undermine our confidence in the word of God by doing what he did in Eden; he sows seeds of doubt and even contradicts Gods' word through false teachers and their 'doctrines of demons'. False teaching and false teachers have their origin in hell and have been the authors of confusion throughout the unfolding history of the Christian Church and unless we stand on the solid rock of Gods' word instead of the ever shifting sand of so-called modern scholarship, we will be unable to stand against the wiles of the devil, which brings us back to this passage in Ephesians and this third item of armour, "and having shod your feet with the preparation of the gospel of peace." (Ch.6:15).

In doing so, and in coming to this item in order to examine it, we need always to bear in mind that the apostles' concern here is not with evangelism where we would expect some form of activity in keeping with that task and which would probably involve our moving forward to engage the sinner. Instead, his concern here is with maintaining and defending our oneness and our unity as Christians. And it is in the light of that concern we are to seek to understand what the apostle is saying to us here since this is a very crucial part of our preparation for this inevitable spiritual conflict before us. As the apostle Paul wrote to the Church in Corinth, "Therefore, my beloved brethren, be steadfast, immovable, always abounding in the work of the Lord, knowing that your labor is not in vain in the Lord." (1 Corinthians Ch. 15:58).

The Lord tells us of the wise man who built his house upon the rock because it was the best foundation on which to build it, since here he could weather the storms that arise from time to time. For the Christian the rock we build on is Christ Jesus as presented in the scriptures. Satan is aware of this and therefore his goal or objective is to move us from this safe position and away from the safety of the solid foundation of His word, to forsake the safety of His truth, to distrust what we once held to be the truth, to abandon our convictions, to cause us to lose our balance and to wrong foot us completely; a very dangerous situation since an army unable to stand is an army unable to fight. It is immobilized, put out of the struggle and thus an easy prey to a powerful enemy.

It is this situation that the apostle is concerned with here. Our enemy has many tactics and devices which he can, and does, employ in order to divide the Christian church. Indeed, we are living in a day when Satan is doing all that he can to strip us of this item of armour in order to undermine our stability and our security. It is vital therefore that we hold fast to the truth for if we do, the truth will hold us fast.

Coming back then to the item itself, it is important to remember that this footwear is the third item in the order employed by the apostle and that even this has something to teach us. As the girdle of truth is a necessary foundation for the armour, and a very necessary item to embrace as we begin to prepare for the battles ahead, so the breastplate of righteousness is not only the evidence and natural outcome of this truth but is the next requirement for the Christian soldier in his, or her, preparation for the forthcoming struggle. Therefore, in keeping with this process we find the apostle turning our attention to the spiritual footwear which, he implies, should be our next concern since it has to do with our ability to stand firm; we are to remain faithful to the truth we have embraced and therefore to the word of God. As we continue to consider these items in the order set before us, we will have cause to return to a consideration of this process. However, there is one more truth associated with this third item that we still need to address, namely, the term the apostle uses here in connection with the footwear; a very necessary part of our 'preparation' is associated with the 'gospel of peace' and our question is , why does he employ this term here? What significance does it have in this passage? Why does the apostle describe it as the gospel of peace and not the gospel of God's grace or the gospel of God's love, etc.?

In seeking an answer to this question, our first observation must simply be to note that the apostle is not thinking here of the gospel as a whole; he is not thinking of the gospel in all its' fullness but has simply singled out one aspect of it, or one result or benefit of it. Indeed, he is directing our attention to a very important effect of the gospel which is essential to our stability and security in the midst of the conflict we are engaged in. I refer, of course, to that word we have yet to consider, the word 'peace'.

There are many words we may associate with the gospel, but it is this word 'peace' that the apostle has chosen here as the one most in keeping with our need as we face our enemy and prepare for his onslaught.

Clearly, the apostle knew in his own experience and in a very personal way the importance of this 'peace' in the midst of all the trials and the sufferings he endured on account of his faithfulness to the gospel and to his Saviour. Indeed, there are a number of examples we can find in the scriptures of this remarkable peace in the lives of Gods' people. Daniel comes to mind along with his three companions, and in spite of the initial failure of the disciples in the storm and at the cross, due to their limited faith prior to Calvary, we see Peter, later on, following the resurrection, asleep in prison prior to what could have been the day of his execution, as well as the apostle Paul and Silas singing in the Philippian jail at midnight after being beaten with rods unlawfully.

Nor is this faith common among men, even Christian men. Like Thomas of old many of us are hard to convince that all will be well. We too would insist upon seeing the nail prints in His hands and feet before we are ready to fall down before Him in order to worship Him as our Lord and our God. For only then can we truly experience the peace of God in all its' wonder. Nor is it enough for us to hear the word of the Lord as the disciples heard it on the very night when He was arrested prior to His death; "Peace I leave with you, My peace I give to you; not as the world gives do I give to you. Let not your heart be troubled, neither let it be afraid." (John Ch. 14:27); a remarkable statement in the light of what our Lord was about to endure.

Two observations we need to make here; first of all, what kind of peace was that peace which our Saviour had at such a time when before Him lay a path of such suffering as no other man could ever contemplate, far less endure!

Secondly, we see that in spite of this offer of peace which the Lord gave to these troubled men, they forsook the Lord and fled when the Saviour was arrested and hid themselves away for fear of the Jews. Not until He rose from the dead did they finally enjoy that peace of which the Lord had spoken. And it is that truly remarkable peace which we too require to know if we are ever to be able to stand as they eventually did.

In the words of that wonderful hymn (that, sadly, we seldom sing today) by Edward Henry Bickersteth wrote in the late 19th Century,

'Peace, perfect peace, in this dark world of sin? The blood of Jesus whispers peace within.'
'Peace, perfect peace, by thronging duties pressed? To do the will of Jesus, this is rest.'
'Peace, perfect peace, with sorrows surging round? On Jesus' bosom nought but calm is found.'
'Peace, perfect peace with loved ones far away? In Jesus' keeping we are safe, and they.'
'Peace, perfect peace, our future all unknown? Jesus we know, and He is on the throne.'
'Peace, perfect peace, death shadowing us and ours? Jesus has vanquished death and all its powers.'
'It is enough: earth's struggles soon shall cease, and Jesus call us to heaven's perfect peace.'

As we are aware, man has sinned against His Creator and has broken His laws. In doing so he has incurred guilt by being both an offence and an affront to God, thus causing Him to be angry. In short, man has stirred up trouble for himself. Indeed, he has aroused the wrath of God against himself, for as we read in Psalm 7:11 "The Lord is angry with the wicked every day." We have incurred His displeasure. As the apostle John tells us in his gospel, "He who believes in the Son has everlasting life; and he who does not believe the Son shall not see life, but the wrath of God abides on him." (Ch. 3:36)

We, on the other hand, are angry with God for giving us laws that we do not like and for telling us off when we break them. Indeed, we are furious that He should plan to punish us for our disobedience. We resent His authority!

As for our relationship with our fellow man, we tend to hate them also. In his letter to Titus the apostle made this observation concerning mankind, "For we ourselves were also once foolish, disobedient, deceived, serving various lusts and pleasures, living in malice and envy, hateful and hating one another." (Titus Ch.3:3)

This situation is a result of our sin. Nevertheless, it is one which is addressed and answered in the message of the gospel, as we see, first of all, in our relationship to the Lord when we receive Him as our Saviour. We see this in the apostle Pauls' letter to the Romans, "Therefore, having been justified by faith, we have peace with God through our Lord Jesus Christ etc." (Ch. 5:1). This is objective peace (which should lead to an inward and subjective peace).

In addition to the above we have the peace referred to in Ephesians Ch.2:14 "For He Himself is our peace, who has made us both one, and has broken down the middle wall of separation, having abolished in His flesh the enmity, that is, the law of commandments contained in ordinances, so as to create in Himself one new man from the two, thus making peace, and that He might reconcile them both to God in one body through the cross, thereby putting to death the enmity. And He came and preached peace, to you who were afar off and to those who were near. For through Him we both have access by one Spirit to the Father." This too is objective in that it has been established by the Lord on the ground of His atonement whether or not we experience this oneness in our day to day relationships with our fellow Christians. After all, when our natural family relationships go through troublesome times it does not change the fact that we are family. So too in the spiritual realm!

However, as with the breastplate of righteousness there are two further areas of concern to be considered here. In the first place we have the objective aspect of this peace which is certain and unchanging for those who are truly saved. And no one can undo what our Saviour has secured by His death.

In addition to this, however, we have another concern. We have the subjective experience of the saints to consider since it is right here our enemy will attack us again and again in order to undermine and overthrow our confidence in God's word and His promises. He knows that he cannot undo what Christ has done. Nevertheless, he will make every effort to unsettle us and to rob us of that peace which is so essential to our souls' wellbeing which, in turn, will have a negative impact upon our witness to the world of sinners surrounding us. We need on such occasions, to put our faith in God's word and not in our own feelings, in His promises and not in our own achievements, or lack of them. This 'gospel of peace' is not only an essential part of our salvation, it is also an essential part of our sanctification and an essential part of our service!

The message then is simple. Gospel unity is only truly found where the truth (which is the foundation of the gospel), and righteousness (the product or desired result of the gospel) are to be found. These should result in each of God's children knowing His marvelous 'peace' which even Satan cannot destroy. However, the gospel of peace can only be effective where these other two are maintained. Where truth and righteousness are absent, true peace will also be absent and unity will not, and cannot, exist. As the apostle wrote to the Philippians, "Be anxious for nothing, but in everything by prayer and supplication, with thanksgiving, let your requests be made known to God; and the peace of God, which surpasses all understanding, will guard your hearts and minds through Christ Jesus." (Phil. Ch. 4:6-7).

Chapter Four: A Good Time to Pause and Reflect

Although my wife and I now live in Dallas, Texas, we were both born and brought up in the country affectionately known as 'Bonnie' Scotland; a very beautiful country, and in spite of the fact that Jean and I would be classed as lowlanders, we also loved the highlands, those more mountainous areas in the north, and the rolling hills of the south. On occasions we would stop on our journeys when we were able, to climb them where we could. In doing so we would often pause on our ascent in order to take in the wonderful scenery, which at times could be quite breathtaking.

Nevertheless, following our wedding on the 25th of May, 1972 we were even more impressed by the sheer grandeur of the Swiss Alps surrounding the area which we had chosen for our honeymoon near Interlaken. Although we often took the chair lifts or the cable cars up the mountains, for obvious reasons, there were occasions when we did some hiking. The higher we climbed the more often we stopped to take in the astonishing views. On our journey through life and in our study of God's word it is also a wise practice to pause now and then to remind ourselves just what our objectives are, our spiritual goals, and to ensure that we are following the right path, that we know where exactly we are going and just how far we have progressed. So too, in our study of this passage at the end of the apostles letter to the Ephesians, it is important to remind ourselves exactly what the goal of the apostle is here, and what exactly he is seeking to say to us in this section of his epistle? The answer I want to give is this, it is a word of advice, it is a most serious word of counsel, it is a word of instruction; indeed, it is a very serious word of warning which we ignore at our peril.

In her book entitled 'A Book of Disasters' Jane Ferguson tells us of the very harrowing account of the town of St. Pierre on the island of Martinique.

'Martinique is one of the Windward Islands, part of the long string of islands, big and small, that we call the West Indies, looped between North and South America in the Caribbean Sea. One of the earth's major volcanic chains runs through them.'

'In 1902 St. Pierre was a busy commercial town, built at the foot of a volcano called Mt. Pelee (named after the Hawaiian goddess of volcanos). No one bothered much about any danger – there had only been a couple of rumblings in the last 300 years.'

'Perhaps that is why the authorities chose quite deliberately to ignore all the clear signs that Mt. Pelee was behaving in an extremely threatening way, and to accuse anyone who suggested evacuation, such as the American Consul, of spreading unnecessary panic.'

'One of the more unpleasant reasons was that an election was due, and the all-powerful but mentally unbalanced governor, and the editor of the main paper who supported him, were so determined that nothing should interfere with the voting that they printed quite false assurances that all was well, and even organized an expedition up the mountain to watch the display.'

'Things hotted up – literally - so much so that they abandoned that idea, but by that time it was too late for most people to get away. The first days of May 1902 were already a nightmare of fissures of boiling mud swallowing plantation workers, of people scalded by steam bursts, of choking endless ash dust, of thousands of enormous ants and centipedes – thirty centimeters long, with pink bellies and violet heads – who had been forced down the mountainside and were attacking animals and humans, of plagues of rats forced up from the sewers choked with volcanic mud, of a tidal wave that smashed into the town, and outbreaks of disease in a town crowded with refugees who had fled there for safety – instead of running away from it.'

'It was already far more ghastly and horrifying than anyone had thought possible, but still nothing was done to evacuate the town. The local priests asked the visiting Vicar – General to order such an evacuation, but he refused to bring the Church into conflict with the State. But having seen the appalling condition of the town for himself, and being terrified of the nightly explosions and noise, he decided there was little he could do and that it was his absolute duty to return home!'

'Unbelievably, then, the town was full – in fact, fuller than usual – when, at 8.02 a.m. on Thursday, May 8th, as people were gathering for Ascension Day Mass, Mount Pelee blew an area roughly ninety metres square out of its side, and sent down on the town a lethal 400-metre-high cloud of fire and gas and ash that wiped out the entire place and everyone in it, and even most of those on board ships in the harbor: 29,933 men women and children.' Only two young men survived due to their being in underground cellars.

An even more serious example still may be found in the first of six volumes on 'The Second World War', penned by Sir Winston Churchill, in the fifth chapter and in his summary found in the closing paragraph, where he wrote, 'We must regard as deeply blameworthy before history the conduct not only of the British National and mainly Conservative Government, but of the Labour–Socialist and Liberal Parties, both in and out of office, during this fatal period. Delight in smooth–sounding platitudes, refusal to face unpleasant facts, desire for popularity and electoral success irrespective of the vital interests of the State, genuine love of peace and pathetic belief that love can be its sole foundation, obvious lack of intellectual vigour in both leaders of the British Coalition Government, marked ignorance of Europe and aversion from its problems in Mr. Baldwin, the strong and violent pacificism which at this time dominated the Labour-Socialist Party, the utter devotion of the Liberals to sentiment apart from reality, the failure and worse than failure of Mr. Lloyd George, the erstwhile great war-time leader, to address himself to the continuity of his work, the whole supported by overwhelming majorities in both Houses of Parliament: all these constituted a picture of British fatuity and fecklessness which, though devoid of guile, was not devoid of guilt, and, though free from wickedness or evil design, played a definite part in the unleashing upon the world of horrors and miseries which, even so far as they have unfolded, are already beyond comparison in human experience.'

The attitude of Sir Winston Churchill was anathema to the pacifists of that time. Nevertheless, the day would come when they would give thanks for his insight and foresight prior to the Second World War. Indeed, their unwillingness to believe what he was saying was clearly one reason why Adolf Hitler got as far as he did and why so many people died in the carnage and destruction that followed the declaration of war in September 1939.

Similar examples of such failure to listen to the words of warning and an unwillingness to believe that such horrific disasters may be about to befall us are not lacking in the unfolding story of the human race. Indeed, they are legion! For example, in this passage of scripture before us we have one such example, have we not? As followers of the Lord Jesus Christ we find ourselves being called to prepare to be engaged in a terrible spiritual conflict with the powers of darkness where so much is at stake; this is a truth that we need to constantly bear in mind as we seek to live for the Lord Jesus Christ amidst so many enemies and so much demonic activity. Like so many politicians prior to World War Two and the residents of St. Pierre, we may not want to hear such a message or to dwell on this fact; nevertheless, to fail to take such an appeal as this one seriously is to be foolish indeed.

Which brings us back to this appeal here at the end of this letter and to the exhortation of the apostle Paul to, as the hymn writer, George Duffield, put it so well in his great hymn, "put on the gospel armour, each piece put on with prayer;" so that, "where duty calls or danger," we'll "be never wanting there." Clearly, the apostle is concerned to impress upon our minds, in this appeal, the seriousness of this issue, of this spiritual warfare which we face as Christians and so now we come to verse sixteen and to the fourth item in the list the apostle brings to our attention, namely, the shield of faith.

Chapter Five: The Shield of Faith

As we see from what the apostle says here, the aforesaid is not the only reason we have for pausing here in our study of these items of armour, for in moving on to this next item to be taken up by the Christian, the apostle introduces it by placing a particular emphasis upon it in the following manner, "above all, taking the shield of faith."

Three items have been referred to thus far, each one making its own contribution to the preparation and protection of the Christian soldier. Indeed, we have even taken note of the order the apostle employs in referring to each of these items since this too must be deemed as important. Nevertheless, at no time did he suggest that any other part of the armour was to be considered of greater importance than the rest, until now that is. At first sight, it may seem to suggest that this is due to an increasing order of importance in the items mentioned. However, there is no other evidence to support this conclusion and therefore we must assume that the apostle is laying a particular emphasis upon this item of armour for a reason or even reasons which he would have us pause to consider, and so we need to look at this item with particular care in order to discover the apostles reason, or reasons, for this comment; and so we need to make a number of observations regarding this particular part of our armour.

To begin with, and at the risk of sounding repetitious, my first remark in seeking to understand the apostles teaching here must be, as noted on a number of occasions thus far, that his concern is not with evangelistic endeavour, but with 'maintaining the unity of the spirit in the bond of peace.' The shield is not required here for aggressive action, so much as being a part of the Christian soldiers' preparation for defensive activity.

Now as we saw in regard to the breastplate of righteousness and the gospel of peace for our feet, the shield of faith refers to a specific aspect or particular use of faith and must not therefore be confused with saving faith for example. It is not that there are different kinds of faith but, rather, that there are various ways in which faith can be and should be employed by the believer from the initial act of trusting in the Lord Jesus Christ for salvation, where faith is given to us as a gift (Ephesians Ch. 2:8), to the living of the Christian life where faith is required on a daily basis.

The faith referred to here, therefore, in the closing section of this same letter is of the same nature as the faith gifted to us at the beginning of the Christian life. It differs only in its' application or use. As it was given, initially, for a different and distinct purpose (the saving of our souls), so in the closing section of this epistle it is to be used for another purpose altogether. On this occasion it is to be used as a shield to protect the one who is already saved from the fiery darts of the devil.

Nevertheless, we would be greatly mistaken if we concluded, as some would appear to have done, that faith is always given to us as a gift. This becomes abundantly clear from a study of the gospels and clearer still from a consideration of the apostles letter to the Hebrews. The very words of the apostle here should leave us in no doubt as to our duty, our responsibility; "above all, taking the shield of faith with which you will be able to quench all the fiery darts of the wicked one."

This is not, therefore, that gift of faith which the Lord bestows upon the sinner in order to justify them, a supernatural gift wrought in us by God's grace; nor is it faith of another kind. Rather, it is faith in a greater measure, faith that is stronger, more mature, a faith which has grown more powerful akin to what we see exemplified in the life of Abraham and many other saints both past and present.

The story of Abraham is a wonderful example of how we are to learn to put our faith in the Lord, both in His word and His Person. Commanded to leave his home, his family and his country, Abram did leave Ur, but his obedience was imperfect. He failed to leave his father and had to wait until after his death before the Lord spoke to him again and led him on. Not that he was fully obedient even yet for we read that his nephew, Lot, went with him. Having reached the land the Lord had promised to give him, a famine arose. Rather than looking to the Lord for guidance and help, Abram chose to go down to Egypt for relief where he asked Sarah not to let them know that she was his wife. Sure enough, she was taken by Pharoah until the Lord intervened. Abram had failed to trust the Lord and thus nearly compromised his wife's moral purity as well as bringing shame and embarrassment upon himself. Nor were Abram and Sarah the only ones to suffer as a result of going down to Egypt. Having amassed larger herds of cattle Abram and Lot needed to separate from one another since the land could not sustain them both in the same region. Given the first choice, Lot lifted his eyes and saw the plain of Sodom and Gomorrah like the land of Egypt. This memory clearly influenced his choice, a decision he may well have deeply regretted in the years that followed; and all because Abram, in a time of famine, acted without seeking the Lords guidance. In times of difficulty and testing we need to have a strong faith and the greater the trial the greater that faith needs to grow and develop. Over the years Abram, whose name was changed by the Lord to Abraham (from 'exalted father' to 'father of a multitude' Genesis Ch.17:1-8), was tested until his faith grew stronger, the climax of this great change being the call to sacrifice his son Isaac testing not only his love for his son, but, more importantly his faith in the Lord. From him nations, kings and a great multitude were to come. That Abraham believed the Lords promise is seen in what he said to the young men who had travelled to the place of sacrifice with them, "Stay here with the donkey; the lad and I will go yonder and worship and we will come back to you."

As referred to above, during His ministry, the Lord had, on a number of occasions, to address some words of rebuke to His disciples regarding their lack of faith. On one occasion, while crossing the Sea of Galilee, a storm arose. The fearful disciples woke the Lord from a deep sleep saying, "Lord, save us. We are perishing!" To which the Lord replied, "Why are you fearful, O you of little faith."

Another example of this lack of faith is also found in the gospels where following the Lords' transfiguration the Lord is approached by a deeply troubled man concerned for his epileptic son. The man had brought his son to the disciples who were unable to deliver the lad. When the disciples asked why they could not deliver the lad, the Lord replied, "because of your little faith."

Perhaps the most notorious example of this condition is to be found at the time of the Lords arrest and crucifiction. The disciples fled! Only the resurrection and the appearance of the risen Lord delivered the disciples from this lack of faith and unbelief. Indeed I feel at this point I must digress for a moment to address yet another concern, a concern that troubled many of our Churches some years ago when, under the influence of the Charismatic movement we were told that the real problem with the Churches of that time was that we were living more like the disciples prior to Pentecost and the coming of the Holy Spirit. We had no power! We, too, needed to experience what was being called 'a second blessing'. We needed to receive the Holy Spirit!

The real problem however, is not that we were bereft of power. What we lacked was faith! As we are told by Luke in his account of the two disciples on the road to Emmaus, when the Lord joined them, they were cast down, they were sad! However, it was not power that they lacked, but faith! As the Lord said to them, "O foolish ones, and slow of heart to believe in all that the prophets have spoken!" (Luke Ch. 24:25). Thomas, one of the twelve, struggled with this issue more than the others it would seem as John relates in his gospel; "Then, the same day, at evening, being the first day of the week, when the doors were shut where the disciples were assembled, for fear of the Jews, Jesus came and stood in the midst, and said to them, 'Peace be with you.' When He had said this, He showed them His hands and His side. Then the disciples were glad when they saw the Lord."

"Now Thomas, called the twin, one of the twelve, was not with them when Jesus came. The other disciples therefore said to him, 'we have seen the Lord.'"

"So he said to them, 'Unless I see in His hands the print of the nails, and put my finger into the print of the nails, and put my hand into His side, I will not believe.'"

"And after eight days His disciples were again inside, and Thomas with them. Jesus came, the doors being shut, and stood in the midst, and said, 'Peace to you!' Then He said to Thomas, 'Reach your finger here, and look at My hands; and reach your hand here, and put it into My side. Do not be unbelieving, but believing." (John Ch.20:19-27).

Nor is this lack of faith an insignificant problem, as the letter to the Hebrews bears witness, for, throughout that letter the apostle is at great pains to encourage them on the one hand, and to warn them on the other, with regard to this whole issue of faith, as the following passages make clear; having extolled the Person of the Lord Jesus Christ and having spoken of the purpose of His coming, he sounds a very serious word of warning. Having drawn attention to the failure of their fathers in the wilderness, he writes, "Beware, brethren, lest there be in any of you an evil heart of unbelief in departing from the living God; but exhort one another daily, while it is called 'today' lest any of you be hardened through the deceitfulness of sin. For we have become partakers of Christ if we hold the beginning of our confidence steadfast to the end, while it is said: 'Today, if you will hear His voice, do not harden your hearts as in the rebellion.' For who, having heard, rebelled? For was it not all who came out of Egypt, led by Moses? Now with whom was He angry forty years? Was it not with those who had sinned, whose corpses fell in the wilderness? And to whom did He swear that they would not enter His rest, but to those who did not obey? So we see that they could not enter in because of unbelief. Therefore, since a promise remains of entering His rest, let us fear lest any of you seem to have come short of it. For indeed the gospel was preached to us as well as to them; but the word that was preached to them did not profit them, not being mixed with faith in those who heard it." (Hebrews Ch.3:12-Ch.4:2).

Later on, having demonstrated the superiority of the Person of Christ to all who had come before Him, and the superiority of His work over theirs, the author comes to the heart of this great appeal, for that is exactly what this letter is, an urgent appeal addressed to the hearts and minds of those early Christians; and this concern for his readers, at the end of chapter ten, forms the introduction to this tremendous chapter on faith, chapter eleven, where the author speaks to the issue which lay at the heart of the problem regarding the bitter struggle they were engaged in. A struggle they had anticipated but not quite in terms of depth and duration, and so it was they had begun to weaken in their resolve to go on and also in their commitment to the gospel itself. The cost and the suffering they were having to endure was far greater than they had been prepared to bear. And so it is the apostle addresses them, "But recall the former days in which, after you were illuminated, you endured a great struggle with sufferings: partly while you were made a spectacle both by reproaches and tribulations, and partly when you became companions of those who were so treated; for you had compassion on me in my chains, and joyfully accepted the plundering of your goods, knowing that you have a better and an enduring possession for yourselves in heaven. Therefore, do not cast away your confidence, which has great reward. For you have need of endurance, so that after you have done the will of God, you may receive the promise: 'For yet a little while, and He who is coming will come and not tarry. Now the just shall live by faith; but if anyone draws back, My soul has no pleasure in him.' But we are not of those who draw back to perdition, but of those who believe to the saving of the soul."

"Now faith is the substance of things hoped for, the evidence of things not seen. For by it the elders received a good testimony. By faith we understand that the worlds were framed by the word of God, so that the things which are seen were not made of things which are visible. By faith Abel offered to God a more acceptable sacrifice than Cain, through which he obtained witness that he was righteous, God testifying of his gifts; and through it he being dead still speaks. By faith Enoch was taken away so that he should not see death, 'and was not found, for God had taken him'; for before he was taken he had this testimony that he pleased God. But without faith it is impossible to please Him, for he who comes to God must believe that He is, and that He is a rewarder of those who diligently seek Him." (Hebrews Ch. 10:32-Ch. 11:6). Here, then, is the great need of those who are the soldiers of Christ.

This epistle written to those early Jewish disciples makes it clear that a doubting of God's word will only lead to a departing from God's ways. Indeed, examples of this abound in scripture. We have already cited the example of Abraham and the sad consequences both in the sorry tale of Lot (from whom came the Ammonites and the Moabites) to which we may also add the example of Abraham and Sarah, the birth of Ishmael and the dreadful legacy this has led to in the story of the two sons of Abraham, Ishmael and Isaac. Unbelief played a part also in the story of Jacob and Esau, the failure of Israel to enter into the land of promise, David's flight from king Saul which led to his being in the camp of the Philistines on the eve of battle against his own people. Indeed, many are the examples we could refer to.

Therefore, we need, above all else, to take up the shield of faith! For, as the apostle goes on to say here, it is with this we "will be able to quench all the fiery darts of the wicked one"; which, in turn, leads us to a consideration of the shield of faith itself, as to its place and as to its purpose in the Christians armour.

Once again it is important to recognise that if the concern of the apostle had been with the task of evangelism, we would expect that the item needed 'above all' would be the sword of the Spirit; however, since the concern of the apostle is with defending ourselves against the attacks of the enemy in his attempts to divide our ranks and to destroy our unity, it is the shield of faith that we need 'above all'!

Due to the importance of this particular item, there are certain questions we might wish to consider here if we are to understand the thinking of the apostle with regard to its place and to its purpose in this spiritual battle; beginning with a very obvious question, what is faith? Is it, as some would suggest, simply belief in something or someone? To which we must reply, with respect to the issue of Christianity, no, it is not merely belief. It does include belief but it is much more than mere belief. It includes trust, it includes confidence and a deep seated conviction, an assurance in the one who exercises that faith.

As we noted earlier on this issue, the faith of the Christian is first and foremost a gift from God. In short, it is supernatural and is the result of the Holy Spirit of God giving to us the gift of spiritual life whereby we are born again (John Ch. 3:1-6). In the words of Hebrews once again, "Now faith is the substance of things hoped for, the evidence of things not seen….By faith we understand that the worlds were framed by the word of God, so that the things that are seen were not made of things which are visible." It becomes clear from this that the faith of the Christian is supernatural as to its origin and as to its nature. And yet it is much more than a mere acceptance of propositions and statements that cannot be verified since the prelude to this position is nothing short of an act of God whereby the one who now believes was spiritually dead. But now, through the work of the Holy Spirit and by the grace of God the one who was dead is now alive again. The faith of the Christian is not merely 'belief', but a deep seated conviction which is the result and product of the new life the Lord has granted to those who once were dead in trespasses and sin. To explain this act of God to those who do not believe and therefore have never experienced a work of grace in their hearts is well nigh impossible for the conviction of the Christian is due entirely to an act of God that takes place under the teaching of the bible, through the word of God as the apostle tells us in his great letter to the Romans, "How then shall they call on Him in whom they have not believed? And how shall they believe in Him of whom they have not heard? And how shall they hear without a preacher? And how shall they preach unless they are sent? …… So then faith comes by hearing, and hearing by the word of God." (Ch.10:14-17).

To be content to be saved by this gift of Gods' grace is to be guilty of a terrible error. It is akin to being born physically (another event or act we do not control or take responsibility for) and then remaining content to be alive while failing to make any effort to nurture or feed the body we now indwell. This would have a very sad ending indeed. We may not be responsible for the act of our birth but we cannot expect to be kept alive or to develop, grow and mature without feeding and nourishing our bodies. So too in the realm of the Spirit! We may not be responsible for our salvation as this becomes ours through an act of God; it is ours as a gift of His grace. Nevertheless we are clearly expected to grow in grace, which also requires us to develop our faith, to deepen that faith, and since faith comes by hearing and hearing by the word of God, it must be by feeding on the truth both in our personal and private study of God's word and in our giving heed to the preaching of God's truth in the context of the gathered Church that we develop and deepen that faith!

One additional and important observation here must be with regard to that well known chapter on faith which we have already referred to, Hebrews chapter eleven, for all too often we have spoken of the remarkable list of those who are mentioned by name in that chapter; "And what more shall I say? For the time would fail me to tell of Gideon and Barak and Samson and Jephthah, also of David and Samuel and the prophets: who through faith subdued kingdoms, worked righteousness, obtained promises, stopped the mouths of lions, quenched the violence of fire, escaped the edge of the sword, out of weakness were made strong, became valiant in battle, turned to flight the armies of the aliens. Women received their dead to life again," etc. Nevertheless, such a chapter, far from encouraging us, would only drive us to despair if, in looking at this great list of achievements, we made the mistake of looking at the list of these well known names and placed our emphasis there, for this would be to be guilty of a grave error indeed for the author is not seeking to lay his emphasis upon the persons named in this passage but upon 'faith' itself! Each reference to this remarkable record of victories begins, not with their names but with the words, "By faith Abel, By faith Enoch, By faith Noah, By faith Abraham, By faith Sarah," etc. The emphasis is upon what faith has accomplished rather than upon those who possessed it.

Now, this is not to say that those men and women referred to in this chapter are not worthy of our attention and admiration; they are, for the faith they exercise here is not saving faith; that, as we have noted already, is the gift of God for which we cannot take any credit at all. The faith exercised in these examples is the faith those Hebrews are expected, and exhorted to pursue once they are saved. However, it would seem to be obvious that it is faith itself that the author is concerned to emphasize here. Indeed, I would suggest that it is very much a question of emphasis since there can be no doubt that what the apostle is concerned to do at this point is to place his emphasis upon the importance of faith and what can be accomplished by those who choose to place that faith in the Lord and in His word.

Furthermore, to understand the concern of the apostle here requires us to narrow this issue of faith even further since we are dealing with a very specific issue, namely, defending the unity of the body of Christ against a very specific aspect of the wiles of the devil, for, as the apostle tells us we are, "above all" to "take the shield of faith with which you will be able to quench all the fiery darts of the evil one." Our faith then, is to function as a shield in order to protect us from 'the fiery darts of the evil one' as he seeks to attack the Christian Church with a single purpose which is to divide those whom God has joined together in the body of Christ!

Chapter Six: The Fiery Darts of The Wicked One

In the light of what has gone before it ought to be obvious by now that what we have here in these verses towards the end of this epistle is not only a description of the Christians armour but a most penetrating, perhaps the most penetrating, analysis of the Christian life to be found in the whole of the New Testament. For just as the book of the Psalms provides us with the most penetrating insight into the heart and mind of the believer in the various circumstances of life, this short passage provides us with yet another penetrating insight, this time, into the life and experience of the believer; into our lives as they are lived from day to day, a life and experience from which none of us are exempt and from which none of us can escape or hope to avoid.

Nor is it without importance or significance that this letter to the Ephesians is believed to be one of the last letters ever written by the apostle Paul as he neared the end of his life and only after he had come through so many difficulties and trials as well as opposition and suffering. As a consequence he had come to look upon the varied circumstances of his life following his experience on the Damascus road, the trials and the troubles he had faced as well as the sufferings he had endured as having spiritual significance. Nothing happens by chance! For behind the things that are seen are the things that are unseen! Behind the visible is the invisible! Behind the hatred of men is the hatred of Satan. And yet, as Christians we need to remember and acknowledge the fact that behind the hand of Satan and of those principalities and powers that desire our destruction is the hand of our God. He is, as the hymn writer (A. C. Ainger 1841-1919) tells us, ever working His purpose out as year succeeds to year and as he goes on to say, "God is working His purpose out, and the time is drawing near, nearer and nearer draws the time, the time that shall surely be, when the earth shall be filled with the glory of God as the waters cover the sea."

This view of his life was not due to some obsession on the part of the apostle Paul or to an over active imagination but to an insight and perception given to him from above and developed through the years in the service of his Lord. Like Joseph the apostle had come to understand that his unbelieving brethren meant it for evil but the Lord meant it for good to the salvation of many including those of his brethren. We are to endure as seeing Him Who is invisible. Not because our salvation depends upon it, but because the witness of the Christian Church, and therefore our usefulness to God as a witness to the world around us, is very much at stake.

Having referred to the shield of faith the apostle now refers to one particular weapon our enemy seeks to employ against us, namely, his 'fiery darts'. This is a weapon which is best used in close combat. The enemy needs to get fairly near to his opponent but not too close lest he is discovered and loses the element of surprise. The dart would sometimes be tipped with poison and could be thrown with great accuracy, the intention being, to get behind his shield. The main objective, of course, would be to strike his opponent where the poison would be most effective and do the most damage.

An example of this is found in the story of Adam and Eve. The very first dart ever thrown was tipped with the poison of unbelief with regard to God's word, the girdle of truth, and this has proved to be the favourite weapon employed against Gods people ever since that fateful day. One important implication to be drawn from all of this ought to be obvious to us all from our study of this particular piece of armour; if faith is needed by the Christian Church "above all", then that which must be dreaded and avoided above all is unbelief! Nothing is more dangerous to the souls of men than this. Nothing is more deadly, nothing can do more damage. Unbelief is costly as Adam and Eve discovered, as did the kings officer in 2 Kings Ch. 7:2, 19 and 20 and so many in Nazareth, since the Lord "could do no mighty works there because of their unbelief." (Matthew Ch. 13:58).

Should we survive that first dart the enemy may very well seek to attack us in regard to the breastplate of righteousness. His goal on this occasion is to aim his dart at the heart of the Christian, to pierce the breastplate of righteousness and to get behind the Christians shield in a moment of carelessness perhaps. To this end he more often than not will employ the world in which we live, either by way of temptation and allurement, or by way of opposition and persecution both of which have met with great success from time to time. Only our love for the Lord Jesus Christ and our love for the brethren provide both an argument and a remedy for such an attack as we see from the message of the apostle John, "Whoever believes that Jesus is the Christ is born of God, and everyone who loves Him also loves him who is begotten of Him. By this we know that we love the children of God, when we love God and keep His commandments. For this is the love of God, that we keep His commandments. And His commandments are not burdensome. For whatever is born of God overcomes the world. And this is the victory that has overcome the world – our faith."

Another dart he uses to great effect is his wicked accusations employed by him to undermine our confidence in the Lord's pardon and forgiveness such as are mentioned in Revelation (Ch. 11:10),

"Then I heard a loud voice saying in heaven, 'Now salvation, and strength, and the kingdom of our God, and the power of His Christ have come, for the accuser of our brethren, who accused them before our God day and night, has been cast down.'" As the apostle tells us in Romans, "What then shall we say to these things? If God is for us, who can be against us?" and be successful that is, "He Who did not spare His own Son, but delivered Him up for us all, how shall he not with Him also freely give us all things? Who shall bring a charge against God's elect? It is God Who justifies. Who is he who condemns? It is Christ Who died, and furthermore is risen, Who is even at the right hand of God, Who also makes intercession for us. Who shall separate us from the love of Christ? Shall tribulation, or distress, or persecution, or famine, or nakedness, or peril, or sword? As it is written, 'For Your sake we are killed all day long; we are counted as sheep for the slaughter.' Yet in all these things we are more than conquerors through Him Who loved us. For I am persuaded that neither death nor life, nor angels, nor principalities, nor powers, nor things present, nor things to come, nor height nor depth, nor any other created thing, shall be able to separate us from the love of God which is in Christ Jesus our Lord." Such confidence this wonderful shield of faith can give us!

Our faith in God's word intact, our righteousness while living in this world accomplished, and our peace within assured, other fiery darts may well be employed to attack our mind, to cause us to neglect God's word or even to neglect the place of prayer. But these are issues that remain to be considered.

Chapter Seven: The Helmet of Salvation or Keeping Our Head!

Like a general in charge of his forces, under attack by an enemy of superior numbers, armed with superior weapons, the Christian must look well to his or her defenses. Satan will come at us from many directions and therefore we must ensure that no area of our spiritual life should be left unguarded or unprotected. And so the apostle Paul continues in the very next verse (verse 17) with yet another exhortation, "And take the helmet of salvation."

Once again the apostle employs the picture of the Roman soldier preparing to defend himself. In doing so he seeks to illustrate spiritual truths and lessons which we will need to employ in the spiritual realm if we are to defend ourselves against the attempts of our enemy to create divisions within the Christian Church in our day. And so we need to begin by asking some very simple and elementary questions such as the following; what is the purpose of the helmet? What significance, in the spiritual realm that is, does that part of the armour and that part of the body play in the protection of the one who wears it? Why is it described as the helmet of 'salvation'? In what way is salvation like a helmet? In what way are they alike? What spiritual lessons can we learn from this comparison to help us in our personal warfare with the "principalities and powers" determined to divide and to destroy us if they can?

Our answer to the first question is quite a simple, straightforward one. The part of the body the helmet is employed to protect, of course, is the head of the soldier. It is here that we encounter the brain wherein resides the reasoning faculties of the man, the place where the decisions are taken by which our actions are determined. It is, if you prefer, the general headquarters of the Christian soldier. Knowing the orders and directives from our Supreme Commander we seek to direct our behavior in accordance with these directives. This is a major target for our enemy who ever seeks to aim his blows at our 'head' in order to confuse us and to disrupt the lines of communication between the Commanding Officer and his troops. A careful study of Church history very soon reveals just how successful this line of attack has proved to be down through the ages. Indeed, as we are all too well aware, in any kind of warfare it is always an important tactic to either feed the opposing army with false information or just to disrupt the enemy's lines of communication. This causes great confusion and undermines morale.

Another important part of the head that needs protection has to be the eyes as any loss of sight would be disastrous. It is important to have good eyesight, good vision, in order to see clearly where the attack of the enemy will come next.

Fortunately, the Christian Church has been greatly blessed with men who have had a particular gift in this area. Like the men of "Issachar who had understanding of the times, to know what Israel ought to do," (1 Chronicles Ch.12:32) there have been many who have been greatly blessed with spiritual understanding and insight as well as the courage to take a stand for the truth regardless of the cost.

The devil is only too well aware that to strike a blow at the head of your opponent is a tactic that must be high on his list of priorities. He not only wishes to disrupt our lines of communication but he also desires to undermine our understanding of the situation, to blur our vision, to ensure that we cannot see anything clearly and to have us become hopelessly confused if not to put us down and even to render us unconscious.

Today we live in the midst of great confusion. We do not seem able to distinguish between friend and foe; we are divided, we are confused while the enemy comes in like a flood, unopposed and unhindered. Which leads me to ask how the helmet of salvation referred to here is able to deliver us from this already widespread predicament. What exactly does salvation have in common with a helmet?

There are those who refer to the apostles comment found in his letter to the Thessalonians where he said, "But let us who are of the day be sober, putting on the breastplate of faith and love, and as a helmet the hope of salvation." (1 Thess. Ch.5:8).

At first sight it may appear to us that these two passages are referring to the same thing. However, I would suggest that a closer look will not support this conclusion, for two reasons. First of all, the issue there is in regard to the return of the Lord and not the protection of our unity or the maintaining of our unity. Furthermore, the breastplate is not compared to righteousness here as it is in Ephesians Ch. 6:14, but to faith and love. In addition, the helmet here is referred to as 'the hope of salvation' and not to salvation itself and so although at first sight it seems to be a similar exhortation to the one we are considering, the fact is they are not the same nor are they dealing with the same issue.

As to what 'salvation' is referring to here, I take it to be exactly that, our salvation in all its glory, with all its benefits and blessings, justification, sanctification, reconciliation, redemption, deliverance from the power of sin, from the penalty of sin, from the guilt of sin and our being transferred from the kingdom of darkness to the kingdom of light, from the captivity of Satan to being a child of the King. Furthermore, it refers to salvation both objectively and subjectively, both what the Lord has done for us and what He has done in us.

Speaking of those who are unsaved and who do not believe the gospel the apostle describes them as those "whose minds the god of this age has blinded, who do not believe, lest the light of the gospel of the glory of Christ, who is the image of God, should shine on them." (2 Cor. Ch. 4:4). Indeed, elsewhere the apostle speaks of Satanic deception, even referring to 'deceiving spirits and doctrines of demons' in 1 Tim. Ch. 4:1. And Satan would love to be able to deceive Christians in the same way but is unable so long as we continue to guard our minds with the helmet of salvation, the knowledge and conviction which the Lord gave to us at the time of our conversion. In this regard our salvation is our salvation! And every time we observe the Lord's supper we are reminded of these great truths which is one very important reason for doing so. Indeed, had the Galatians worn this helmet they would not have been so quick to forsake their loyalty to the gospel of God's grace, nor would this state of affairs been repeated prior to the period of the Reformation requiring so many to engage in that great spiritual, and oft times physical, conflict which claimed the lives of so many of God's saints.

At the beginning of that great letter to the Hebrews we have a solemn reminder and appeal where the author addresses this very concern, "Therefore we must give the more earnest heed to the things we have heard, lest we drift away. For if the word spoken through angels proved steadfast, and every transgression and disobedience received a just reward, <u>how shall we escape if we neglect so great a salvation,</u> which at the first began to be spoken, and was confirmed to us by those who heard Him, God also bearing witness both with signs and wonders, with various miracles, and gifts of the Holy Spirit, according to His own will?" (Ch. 2:1-4).

An understanding of our own salvation is crucial to our maturity and growth as Christians as the apostle Peter warns us in the opening chapter of his second epistle for, having appealed to them to give all diligence and add to their faith virtue, etc. he goes on to say, "For he who lacks these things is shortsighted, even to blindness, and has forgotten that he was cleansed from his old sins." (Ch. 1:9).

The main lesson from the above is, surely, that no Christian can ever afford to wander far from the cross since it is in the message of the cross alone that we find the only answer to our own sinful condition and to the wicked accusations of our enemy. Indeed, only here can we find an answer to the accusations of our own conscience.

Chapter Eight: The Sword of The Spirit

In this appeal to the Christians of his day, urging them to stand against the wiles of the devil and his wicked attempts to divide us, we have now considered five items of armour the Christian will need to acquire if we are going to be able to do so. Only one more item remains to be acquired, one final piece of equipment before we can be ready for the struggle that lies ahead, namely, that which is described as 'the sword of the Spirit'. As we can immediately see, this item is very different from all the others inasmuch as it is the only item that can be properly be described as being a weapon. And yet we must not make the mistake of thinking at this point that the apostle is moving from a consideration of the Christians defensive position to a consideration of his offensive position. The sword is listed here under those items which the Christian is to employ in his defense against the wiles of the devil for it is important to remember the command of the Lord and His purpose as stated in verse 13; "Therefore, take up the whole armour of God, that you may be able to withstand in the evil day, and having done all, to stand."

The soldier who is under attack would be ill prepared to meet the onslaught of the enemy if all he had to rely on were the items of armour we have already considered thus far. Without his sword it would only be a matter of time before the enemy chopped away at his defenses. We must also have a weapon to parry the blows of our enemy, a sword of the finest steel no less. And such a sword the Christian has, one which is tried and true and of which there is none better.

Before we consider how this item of armour is to be employed by the Christian soldier, however, we need to look more closely at the weapon itself in order to consider the material of which it is composed and to admire its weight and its balance. Only then will we realise just how perfectly suited it is to its purpose. Unlike our comments on the shield of faith, we have no need to limit this item in any way. On this occasion we must widen our application to take in the whole of scripture. Each passage, each chapter, each truth is to be used by the soldiers of Christ. As the apostle put it in his letter to young Timothy, "All scripture is given by inspiration of God, and is profitable for doctrine, for reproof, for correction for instruction in righteousness, that the man of God may be complete, thoroughly equipped for every good work." (1 Tim. Ch. 3:16–17). Each passage, each chapter, each truth may be employed by the soldiers of Christ to parry the blows of the enemy and used in our defense.

As to why the apostle described it as the sword 'of the Spirit', we may deduce at least two obvious reasons.

First of all, it is called the sword of the Spirit because He is the One Who fashioned it, He is the One Who provides it, the Master craftsman Who forged it on the anvil of truth. As Peter tells us in his second letter, "prophecy never came by the will of man, but holy men of God spoke as they were moved by the Holy Spirit."(Ch. 1:21).

Secondly, it is called the sword of the Spirit not only because He supplies it for us but because He is the One Who applies it to us. As the author of the letter to the Hebrews tells us, "For the word of God is living and powerful, and sharper than any two-edged sword, piercing even to the division of soul and spirit, and of joints and marrow, and is a discerner of the thoughts and intents of the heart. And there is no creature hidden from His sight, but all things naked and open to the eyes of Him to whom we must give account." (Hebrews Ch.4:12-13). And many a sinner has been arrested in their sinful and even wicked pursuits by the message contained within this book. In the hands of the Holy Spirit the message of this book has transformed the lives of millions of sinners while so many remain in darkness. As the Lord said to His disciples prior to His departure, "These things I have spoken to you while being present with you. But the Helper, the Holy Spirit, whom the Father will send in My name, He will teach you all things, and bring to your remembrance all things that I said to you." (John Ch.14:25-26).

From cover to cover the scriptures are marked by the same divine impression. Whether in the record of history or in the area of prophecy, in the moral, social or spiritual precepts, all require a similar verdict, this is not the work of men but, like the message given to Belshazzar in the book of Daniel, is none other than the finger of God.

As we noted above, this is a weapon that the Holy Spirit wishes to place in the heart of Gods children in order to wage the battle within, for our struggle against the devil must be fought here first. As we read in Psalm 119:9-11, "How can a young man cleanse his way? By taking heed according to Your word. With my whole heart I have sought You; Oh, let me not wander from Your commandments! Your word I have hidden in my heart, that I might not sin against You."

However, the Lord not only desires to write His word upon our hearts, He also desires to place His word into our hands, as we can see here from this passage. He would give us this sword in order that we might use it to defend ourselves against the attempts of our enemy to create division within the ranks of Gods people.

As the apostle Paul wrote to young Timothy, "Be diligent to present yourself approved to God, a worker who does not need to be ashamed, rightly dividing the word of truth.

Of course, not even a master swordsman can teach or train a man who is lazy, a man who has no desire to learn or to make the effort to study the art of swordsmanship. A point worth making in a day like today when we hear so many crying, 'peace, peace,' when there is no peace; perhaps the reason why so many Churches are so weak and ineffective today. Churches are full of those who willingly leave the fighting to others or else Christians are too busy fighting one another to realise that they are doing the devil's work for him. We are bereft of insight, understanding, wisdom, unable to distinguish between truth and error and thus unable "to contend for the faith once delivered to the saints", in part, because we are unable to identify what that 'faith' is.

From the outset it has been my aim to show that the great concern of the apostle in this letter to the saints in Ephesus is the unity of the Christian church and that a very real part of the purpose of Jesus Christ's coming was not only for the saving of individual sinners but the healing of that division created by sin between God and man, and between man and his fellow man. Therefore, although the sword of the Spirit, referred to here in the closing verses of this epistle, may seem to be for the purpose of attacking as well as for defense, I still maintain that the concern here for its use is a more limited one, namely, to enable us to stand! As the apostle tells us in the short passage, we are to "put on the whole armour of God, that" we "may be able to stand against the wiles of the devil" (verse 16); "Therefore take up the whole armour of God that you may be able to withstand" (defensive) "in the evil day, and having done all to stand.

Stand therefore etc" (verses 13 and 14). None of these statements support an offensive position!

We are to be His witnesses to the ungodly, a lamp in a dark place, a city on a hill that cannot be hid, a city of refuge to which the awakened may flee; Satan cannot afford to ignore us and will ever seek to destroy us or at the very least destroy our witness; and as the Lord parried the blows of the devils temptations in the wilderness with the sword of the Spirit, so too, we must learn to handle the word of truth, the sword of the Spirit, as our Saviour has given us an example.

There are two other letters that the apostle wrote that sound a particular warning to those who live at the end of this age, both of which he sent to young Timothy. "But the Spirit expressly says that in latter times some will depart from the faith, giving heed to deceiving spirits and doctrines of demons, speaking lies in hypocrisy, having their own conscience seared with a hot iron, etc." (1 Timothy Ch. 4:1-2) and "But know this, that in the last days perilous times will come. For men will be lovers of themselves" etc. "But you must continue in the things which you have learned and been assured of, knowing from whom you have learned them, and that from childhood you have known the holy scriptures, which are able to make you wise for salvation through faith which is in Christ Jesus."

"All scripture is given by inspiration of God, and is profitable for doctrine, for reproof, for correction, for instruction in righteousness, that the man of God may be complete, thoroughly equipped for every good work." (2 Timothy Ch. 3:1-2, 14-17).

Three observations we can make from these verses and the letters from which they have been taken. First of all we see that there will be:-

[1]. A Deception Which is Fatal:- For some men will think that they have the truth when in fact they will have been taught by those who have been inspired, not by the Holy Spirit but by those whom the apostle describes as 'deceiving spirits.' They will be nothing less than 'doctrines of demons.

In the twenty third chapter of Matthew we find one of the most scathing denunciations of the false teachers ever given by the Lord Jesus, "But woe to you, scribes and Pharisees, hypocrites! For you shut up the kingdom of heaven against men; for you neither go in yourselves, nor do you allow those who are entering to go in. Woe to you, scribes and Pharisees, hypocrites! For you devour widows' houses, and for a pretense make long prayers. Therefore you will receive greater condemnation."

"Woe to you, scribes and Pharisees, hypocrites! For you travel land and sea to win one proselyte, and when he is won, you make him twice a son of hell as yourselves." (Ch. 23:13-15). See also verses 14 -39.

And as we see, this deception which is fatal is based upon:

[2]. A Doctrine Which is False:- For in short, what they are receiving as truths are nothing less than doctrines of demons and anyone who has tried to persuade Roman Catholics, Jehovah's Witnesses, Mormons and the like will soon realise that these doctrines are not the doctrines of men they are dealing with but the teaching of the devil himself. They are often doctrines which appeal to the minds,

the thinking and the reasoning faculties of man. They are often subtle, appealing to his fallen nature. All of which will inevitably lead to -

[3]. A Departure From The Faith: Which is why the New Testament is full of teaching on this issue. Not only does the Lord have much to say on this issue, the letters of the apostles, Peter and Paul have much to say about false teachers and the effect of their teaching. Some of the strongest words of condemnation are reserved for them and for their doctrines.

The areas of concern should be obvious to us all. Although we could furnish a much longer list I would mention just five areas where we must expect to face the opposition and lies of our enemy. First of all,

[1]. We need to know the truth about God. Had Adam and Eve understood this they would never have brought such evil and misery upon themselves or on all who have descended from them. Their first mistake was listening to his lie, 'you shall not die'. He lies about Gods' character, His holiness, His love, His mercy, His patience, His promises, etc.

[2]. We need to know the truth about sin. We need to know the commandments of God and the consequences of not keeping them. We cannot afford to underestimate the power of sin or its' potential to ruin our lives.

[3]. We need to know the truth about salvation. We cannot afford to be guilty of any error here. Satan will ever seek to question our own salvation, to doubt the promises of God, for if he can make us go

astray on this vital issue he will almost certainly render us useless in our witness to others.

[4]. We need to know the truth about the world in which we live. Not so much the physical realm although there are some important truths with regard to this whole subject. What is more important however is the spiritual condition of man, of those amongst whom and with whom we live our lives from day to day.

What the apostle tells us in his second letter to the Corinthians is very helpful here; "but even if our gospel is veiled, it is veiled to those who are perishing, whose minds the god of this world has blinded, who do not believe." (Ch. 4:3-4).

[5]. We need to know the truth about the Lord Jesus Christ above all else. We need to know about His deity, His humanity, His Person as Prophet, Priest and King. We need to know about His birth, His life, His sufferings and His death just to mention a few issues we need to consider.

There was a time when the Holy Spirit put this sword of truth into the hands of men and yet our enemy sought to remove it. Nevertheless, as the Lord told Elijah, when he thought that he was the only one left, He had many in Israel who had not bowed the knee to Baal. And although it appeared (for there were many who had the scriptures and who treasured its' truths) to have been forgotten, the Reformation brought the truths of Gods' word before the world of that day. It did not happen without much suffering however, and we who are alive today and have the scriptures so available to us owe a debt of gratitude to those who stood their ground and gave their lives to pass on the truths of Gods' word to us.

Chapter Nine: Praying Always With All Prayer

Although the apostle has completed his description of the Christians armour he has not completed the list of duties which we must consider as vital for the Christian in preparation for the spiritual conflict before us. One more exhortation is required, namely, what we read in verse eighteen, "praying always with all prayer and supplication in the Spirit, being watchful to this end with all perseverance and supplication for all the saints – and for me", etc. Nor is this an afterthought tagged on to the instructions already given. It may well have an importance greater than anything else he has said to us thus far. A number of very important lessons can, and need to be, learned from this final appeal by the apostle here, not least of which is that having obeyed the exhortations thus far, we do not think that we are now ready to face the enemy, or that we are now equipped for the spiritual battle that most certainly awaits us. Not at all! You and I are no match for the enemy of our souls. Yes, we must do all that we can, we must take seriously the need to be clothed in the armour that the Lord provides. However, once we have done all that we can, we must seek the Lord in prayer since it is only in His strength we will be able to fight the good fight of faith with any hope of success. There must be a looking to the Lord for help in the battle.

Even with all the armour the Lord provides for our protection we are still no match for the principalities and powers of darkness. Yes, he is a defeated foe; his doom is certain, and his power is broken to a very large degree; his days are numbered, and yet, even in this weakened state, he is still too powerful for us and therefore the dangers we face cannot and must not be underestimated. The damage he can do is still significant. Clothed as we are in the armour our Saviour has provided for us we are still no match for his craft and cunning. We need to stay near to our Captain in order to hear His commands, His directions and His encouragements. Indeed, at this point I could cite many a General, King or Commander and the address they gave to their troops on the eve of battle to strengthen their resolve and to encourage them for the coming conflict. Their words and their very presence inspired their troops!

So, too, we need to be reminded that the battle is not ours but the Lords, the strength is not ours but the Lords, and the victory, when achieved, is not ours but the Lords!

However, to consider leaning upon the Lord in prayer while failing to take unto ourselves the armour provided would not be wisdom but presumption and any soldier foolish enough to enter the battlefield with only his belief that the Lord will protect him must not expect to leave the battlefield unharmed or uninjured, assuming that he leaves it at all. Trusting in Gods sovereignty is not enough if we neglect our human responsibility. There is an important relationship between Gods promises and Gods precepts.

Satan's objective is a simple one; he desires to be the ruler of this world, to rid the world of everything and anything that is godly or Christ like. Once a servant of God, created to do His bidding, he is now the most wicked of all Gods' creatures. He desires to usurp the authority of God which led to the fall of man in Eden. He is now the god of this world and will stop at nothing to overthrow Gods' plan of redemption, even to the tempting of the Lord Jesus to avoid the way of the cross. "Again the devil took Him up on an exceedingly high mountain and showed Him all the kingdoms of the world and their glory. And he said to Him, 'All these things I will give You if You will fall down and worship me.'" (Matthew Ch. 4:8-9).

For the moment he is the ruler of this world and will use any and all means to hold onto his position. Unfortunately for him, the Lord Jesus has already given His life to purchase both for the world and all of those he has redeemed from the devil by His blood, and as we see in the book of the Revelation, the day will come when the Lord will take the scroll to open its seals, in order to claim this world as rightfully His.

For the moment the Lord is calling to Himself all those whom He has purchased by His blood, reconciling them first of all to Himself, and then reconciling them to one another in His body, the Christian Church, since it is through them that the Lord bears witness to the world as to His presence and as to His purpose in providing the gospel message by which sinners can be saved. We are now to be the means through which the Lord reveals Himself to the world. And this Satan both hates and opposes with all of his might and with all of his cunning which is the reason why the apostle not only makes his appeal for unity throughout this epistle but also makes this special appeal in this final chapter and in these closing verses of this epistle.

As the Christian Church flourishes, so the rage of Satan increases. He is engaged in a most spiteful vendetta against his creator. He hates the Church since through it God makes His presence felt in what Satan considers is his world. Therefore, he must oppose it, he must do all that he can to destroy it using every evil device he can employ. False teaching, false teachers, compromise, temptation, violence and persecution, sowing tares amongst the wheat, and any other wicked device will be employed to destroy the Church and its' witness. Any way he can he will attack it to render its witness useless. For this reason we need, not only to take unto ourselves the armour of God but also, having done that, we must give ourselves to prayer and cast ourselves upon the Lord due to the fact that we still stand in need of Gods' help. We cannot and must not try to overcome his attacks on our own. Let us recall what happened to the seven sons of Sceva (Acts Ch.19:11-17).

As we noted already, let us not trust to our praying while we fail to prepare. We must first don the armour for only then will we be entitled to pray for help in the battle. And let us remind ourselves that the purpose the apostle has in mind here for our praying is for the unity and fellowship of the Christian Church. As for the phrase, 'praying always', we are reminded ever to be on our guard as the devil never takes a rest.

I believe that someone once wrote, 'the devil trembles when he sees the weakest saint upon his knees.' It is this he is most afraid of, that men should call upon the Lord.

Satan does not like the truth. Nevertheless, let Gods' people be girded with the truth if they must, wear the breastplate of righteousness if they will, have their feet steadied by Gods' peace if they so desire, take up the shield of faith if they insist, wear the helmet of salvation and take the sword of the Spirit if that is what they want to do, but, give yourselves to prayer? No! Anything but that!

The Christian soldier the devil can cope with as long as he is not in touch with his (or her) Commander-in-chief. This exhortation to be in constant touch with the Lord is without doubt the most difficult part of the Christian's duty as it is also the most important. The flesh remaining in us resents it, and even resists it, since it is the ultimate step in humility and the most useful part of our Christian service.

In the story of our decline the first chapter is always the same, the place of prayer is neglected and finally forsaken. But let a Christian, let a church, get on their knees before the Lord, cry out to Him for help, look to Him for power and lean on Him for strength and you can be assured, the powers of hell shall be thrown into confusion!

Chapter Ten: Supplication For All The Saints

A very wise man once said, "A man who isolates himself seeks his own desire; he rages against all wise judgement." (Proverbs Ch. 18:1). Nevertheless, the desire to be independent and self sufficient in man is very strong indeed. This much admired sentiment was made the subject of a popular song sung by Frank Sinatra some years ago entitled, "My Way." Such an attitude is much admired by the man of the world whereas those who need others, who feel they cannot go it alone and who depend upon others, are looked upon as weak and tend to be despised. The one who is able to go it alone is often seen as the hero; he is admired by others and is treated as being a true 'man', one who stands out among men; one reason, I suggest, why so many people reject and even despise the Christian gospel since it embraces a view which is diametrically opposed to such an attitude. Man was not created by the Lord to go it alone.

Those who embrace such a view are guilty of misunderstanding and of misrepresenting the biblical message. It does not make man weak, it merely declares that they are so; that he has been deceived, that he has been taken captive by one who is far more powerful and far more subtle than he is. Man is a prey to his own desires and a slave to his many lusts. He is weak and and prone to fall to temptation. We stand in need of a deliverer, one who is far more powerful than he who holds us captive. And even once we are saved we continue to need the Lord. We need to rely upon Him for wisdom, strength, guidance and protection until we are finally removed from this scene of conflict, this field of battle; one reason why we need to be praying always with all prayer and supplication in the Spirit.

When we bow the knee in prayer we are seeking to give God His rightful place and we are recognizing Him as our rightful Ruler. As far as Satan is concerned this is treachery of the very worst kind. For this reason we will find that it is here we will meet with the greatest opposition of all. The various items of Christian armour we can wear, if we must, but, to continue to give ourselves to prayer to our Father in heaven? No, it cannot be allowed and must be stopped at any cost! It is here that the struggle becomes intense. The Christian soldier Satan can handle but only so long as the Commander-in-Chief is absent, ignored or forgotten.

In bringing this appeal for prayer to a conclusion, perhaps another phrase might be worth considering. Having added to what he has said on the Christian armour, "praying always with all prayer and supplication," he then added this phrase, "in the Spirit." For the danger here is this, that when we face all kinds of problems and opposition both in the world and from the world we then fail to look behind 'the world' to see exactly who it is we are dealing with. We need to remember what the apostle said earlier which is, we wrestle not against flesh and blood alone, but against principalities and powers and the rulers of the darkness of this age.

That this wrestling is indeed against the spiritual hosts of wickedness is no more obvious or apparent than at this very point, when we seek to come to the Lord in prayer. If ever there was a Christian duty which ought to be the easiest and most natural of them all, surely it is praying. And yet it is an undisputed fact that in no other duty do we find ourselves struggling and battling to engage in more than in prayer. We feel tired, we feel weary, our minds are hard to control, our thoughts are easily distracted, or disturbed, or we begin to think of all the other things we need to do. We conclude that we are wrestling with flesh and blood when the real problem is that we are engaged in a spiritual warfare with an enemy we cannot see. And Satan fears the performance of this duty more than any other since here is where God can be invoked to come to our aid when we are oppressed. Like the school bully or an older brother or sister taking advantage of us when we are small, they soon run away when we start calling for our Father. Nothing so stirs the Almighty as the cry of His child in distress. Prayer, real earnest prayer, is the single greatest threat to Satans' rule and influence when directed aright. As the old saying puts it, 'the devil trembles when he sees the weakest saint upon his knees.' And so it is the apostle exhorts us to pray "always with all prayer and supplication in the Spirit, being watchful to this end with all perseverance and supplication for all the saints" etc. (Ch. 6:18).

We may be reminded here of an occasion when, in the garden of Gethsemane, prior to His arrest and crucifiction, the Lord took Peter, James and John apart from the others. We read that, "He began to be sorrowful and deeply distressed. Then He said to them, 'My soul is exceedingly sorrowful, even to death. Stay here and watch with Me.' He went a little farther and He fell on His face, and prayed, saying, 'O My Father, if it is possible, let this cup pass from Me; nevertheless, not as I will, but as you will.' Then He came to the disciples and found them sleeping, and said to Peter, 'What! Could you not watch with Me one hour? Watch and pray, lest you enter into temptation. The spirit indeed is willing, but the flesh is weak.'" (Matthew Ch. 26:37-41).

Prayer is not easy on occasions, even when we are willing to pray. Only a little while before the disciples had spoken of their resolve to suffer with the Lord, yes, and even die for him if required to. But desert Him? Never! Forsake Him? Certainly not! And yet when asked to watch with Him for an hour, to stay awake with Him? And we see how they failed. In Marks' account we read, after yet another failure, "He found them asleep again, for their eyes were heavy; and they did not know what to answer Him." (Mark Ch. 14:40). Nevertheless, it has to be noted that this is not hypocrisy but weakness. They may appear to be the same but they are not. Indeed, Luke tells us that they were "sleeping from sorrow." (Ch.22:45). When our hearts are heavy and our souls are sorrowful we find it almost impossible to perform our spiritual duties. Jonah and Elijah were both found asleep due to the fact, like the disciples in Gethsemane, they could not understand what the Lord was doing at this point in their lives. In the words of 'Bow The Knee', "and when you can't understand the purpose of His plan, in the Presence of your King, bow the knee!"

What a transformation we find in these men following the resurrection. Now they understood what the Lord had come to do! Now they saw 'the purpose of His plan.' No longer were they sleeping for sorrow! For now they could see!

Conclusion

There are two errors that have ever been prevalent among men. The first is to fail to see the Hand of God in all the circumstances of our lives; to look upon the chain of events that make up our experience in life as no more than random, disconnected happenings that have no real significance or importance in and of themselves. We see life as a collection of events where sometimes good, sometimes evil has the upper hand.

Sad to say, amongst the true saints of God in every age this view has been encountered and accepted. Oh, there are, of course, certain times, in certain ages regarding certain events in the life of the Church when the Hand of God may be seen. However, for the most part we carry on our daily lives as though the spiritual realm was not there or at least was not very easy to discern. Sad to say, the eye of faith has often been conspicuous by its absence, our spiritual senses dulled to the point that we are now as unaware of what is going on around us as was the young servant of Elisha who, seeing the army round about Dothan, said, 'Alas, my master! What shall we do?' and for whom the prophet interceded, "'Lord, I pray, open his eyes that he may see.' Then the Lord opened the eyes of the young man, and he saw." (2 Kings Ch. 6:17).

Sometimes I think that an ignorant lout can see as much of God in the events around us as we can and that the only difference between us is that we hope that perhaps, some day, somewhere, somehow God may make Himself known to the world once again. That God is there, we are convinced; that He is here, we are not so sure.

Another error, akin to this, is that we do not take the presence and activity of Satan as seriously as we should. For, although we are warned about him and his activities, we often fail to remember that he can come at us, as a roaring lion seeking to devour or as an angel of light seeking to deceive and his goal is ever the same which is to defy his Creator, to divide His people, and to destroy His Church.

Here, then is our duty; "Finally, my brethren, be strong in the Lord and in the power of His might. Put on the whole armour of God, that you may be able to stand against the wiles of the devil. For we do not wrestle against flesh and blood, but against principalities, against powers, against the rulers of the darkness of this age, against spiritual hosts of wickedness in heavenly places. Therefore, take up the whole armour of God, that you may be able to withstand in the evil day, and having done all, to stand."

"Stand therefore, having girded your waist with truth, having put on the breastplate of righteousness, and having shod your feet with the preparation of the gospel of peace; above all, taking the shield of faith with which you will be able to quench all the fiery darts of the wicked one. And take the helmet of salvation, and the sword of the Spirit, which is the word of God; praying always with all prayer and supplication in the Spirit, being watchful to this end with all perseverance and supplication for all the saints!" (Ephesians Ch. 6:10-18). And may our duty be our delight!

Printed in Great Britain
by Amazon